# Is Gender
# Fluid?

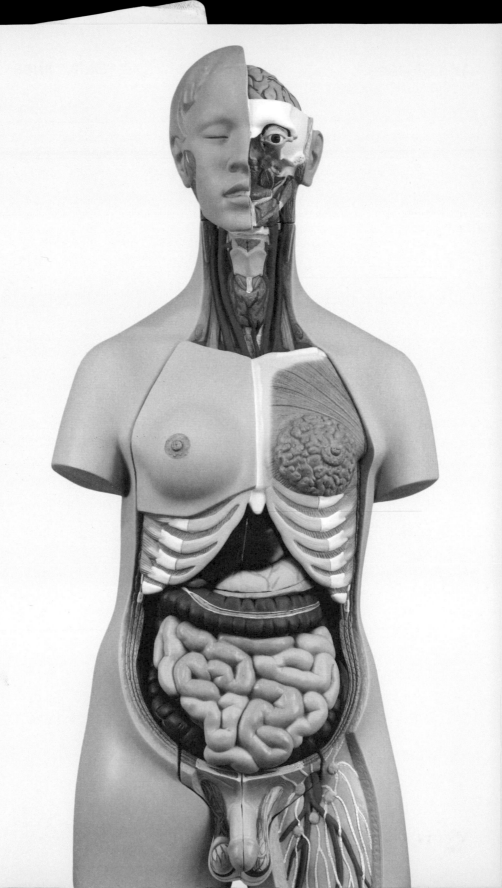

# Is Gender Fluid?

## A primer for the 21st century

Over 160 illustrations

Thames & Hudson

General Editor:
Matthew Taylor

# Contents

# Introduction

A

In its exploration of different understandings and practices of gender, this book examines the meaning of gender itself. As will become clear, the question 'What is gender?' is not at all straightforward. In this book, for example, the term 'sex' generally refers to biological characteristics, whereas 'gender' addresses social and cultural factors.

The relationship between sex and gender is complex, and in fact there exist several starkly different ways of understanding gender.

For some people, gender derives from the biological, reproductive characteristics of sex – that is to say, from the physical, hormonal and chromosomal differences that, they argue, definitively separate male from female. For others, gender is an expression of social norms – a combination of the behaviours, roles and expectations through which a society defines

women and men. Many people see gender
as a combination of these biological and social
factors. But today, an increasingly large group
of people say that gender is not hard-wired
and can be understood and expressed in
a far more diverse range of ways.

In addition, the work of scientists such as Anne Fausto-Sterling
(b. 1944) and Cordelia Fine (b. 1975) has highlighted that some of the
physical and physiological differences between the sexes are not
as clear-cut as we might think. From any of these perspectives,
gender may be understood to be somehow mutable or malleable
– or, to put it another way, gender might be thought of as fluid.

# The idea of gender fluidity suggests that gender is not fixed by biology, but shifts according to social, cultural and individual preference.

A   Traditional gender roles
in the nuclear family are
represented in a Nestlé
magazine advertisement
from the 1960s.
B   Trans women pose
in a hotel room in San
Francisco, California, in
1981. Despite increasing
recognition, transgender
people were classified by
the American Psychiatric
Association in 1980 as
having 'gender identity
disorder'.

B

A

In order to understand this more easily, we might imagine gender as a combination of three factors. Body, or physicality, comprises the reality of each person's body, how they experience it and how others interact with that person based on their body. This physical aspect of gender interacts with gender identity and gender expression. A person's gender identity can remain fixed or can fluctuate over time; can be aligned with or be in contrast to the sex they are assigned at birth; and can be articulated through or contradicted by their gender expression.

**Gender identity** refers to each person's internal sense of being male, female, a combination of the two, or neither; it is a core part of who people know themselves to be.

**Gender expression** is how a person presents their gender to the world, and also how the world interacts with and shapes their gender. This is related to gender roles and how society enforces conformity to those roles.

**Genderfluid** people experience their gender identity as changing over time or between different situations, and may not feel restricted to any one gender identity.

**Genderflux** people experience their gender identity as more or less intense at different times.

**Non-binary** describes any gender identity or expression outside the categories of male and female.

In recent years, terms such as 'genderfluid' or 'genderflux' have gained a foothold in the public consciousness. The idea that gender is non-binary has become more prevalent, and gender-diverse people have gained increasing visibility. Terms such as 'gender queer' and 'agender' are sometimes used to describe experiences and identities not captured by traditional binary definitions of man or woman. Many people identify across the categories of male and female; others state that their gender identity has shifted over time.

Gender is pervasive. It structures our lives in fundamental ways, impacting everything from the activities we are encouraged to enjoy and the behaviours we are expected to display as children, to the subjects we study as young people, to the occupations we enter and the responsibilities we undertake as adults. Yet we are often unaware of its effects.

A **gender-diverse** person does not conform to their society's norms or values when it comes to their gendered physicality, gender identity, gender expression or a combination of these factors. This is a wide category, encompassing a huge variety of people, practices and experiences.

**Gender queer**, like gender non-binary, describes someone whose gender identity does not sit within the social norms of masculine or feminine, but in between or outside these binaries.

**Agender** people identify as having no gender, or feel that their gender is absent or neutral.

A   Part of the Israel Defense Forces, the mixed Caracal infantry battalion is one of three full combat units that include both male and female soldiers.
B   Although the numbers of male midwives are on the increase at Westmead Hospital in Sydney, Australia, in 2017 female midwives there still outnumbered male midwives by 327 to 5.

A

**Inclusive writing** in French aims to neutralize grammatical gender by including both gendered forms in plurals for mixed groups. For example, a group comprising male and female voters, currently 'électeurs', would become 'électeur.rice.s'.

**Embodiment** is the experience and the fact of living in one's body. It relates both to the way a person experiences their body in the context of societal expectations, and also to the way those expectations influence their body.

The workings of gender are key to our identities, intimate relationships, everyday experiences, and social and cultural positioning, but they are often imperceptible. They operate not only as an external component that organizes our lives, but also as an influence on how we imagine the possibilities of our lives, and the lives of those around us. To alter the way we think about gender is to change one of the fundamental ways in which we classify ourselves, other humans, animals and, in some languages and cultures, everyday objects and the words we use to describe them. In French, for example, adjectives are grammatically gendered depending on the gender of the noun they describe, and the default noun gender for a group containing one male is masculine, even when the rest of the group is made up of females. This has led to controversy, with activists campaigning for inclusive writing, incorporating both the masculine and feminine forms when referring to mixed-gender groups.

# Understandings, and thus practices, of gender have never been consistent.

The ways in which gender is experienced in everyday life emerge from different historical, social and cultural frameworks. Traits seen to be typically masculine or feminine have changed greatly over time; what is customary for a man or woman in one country may be seen as unacceptable in another.

Consider what is typical or acceptable behaviour for a woman in Britain in the 21st century, a woman in Britain in the 18th century or a woman in Saudi Arabia in either century. Within the same society, even, different communities have divergent ideas around the norms and values of gender. It is entwined with other social categories, such as race, social class, sexuality and embodiment. The ways in which we are socially positioned through other methods of categorizing and systems of power underwrite how we are socially positioned through gender.

A　In this illustration titled
*The Macaroni Painter,
or Billy Dimple sitting
for his Picture* (1772),
from *Social Caricature in
the Eighteenth Century*,
a painter in macaroni
dress portrays a fellow
macaroni or dandy in
a satire on exaggerated
fashions of the day.
The macaronis were
known for their choice
of clothing, which was
seen as effeminate.

B　These prints of 18th-
century male Parisian
fashion, from the
Metropolitan Museum
menswear collection
1790–1829, indicate
the wearing of corsets
by men.

B

The theory of intersectionality, developed by legal feminist scholar Kimberlé Crenshaw (b. 1959) to analyse the ways in which systems of oppression overlap, is important in recognizing how gender is connected to other structural positions, such as social class and race. The history of working-class women, for example, shows that gender roles are constructed through understandings and experiences of social class. Similarly, the twin categorizing systems of race and gender can work together to oppress minorities in either arena, or both.

Intersectionality takes account of the fact that society's expectations of a woman, man or non-binary person, the possibilities open to them, and the understandings of the relationships between these categories are all shaped by culture. Culture informs gender relations, which act as a central organizing principle of society, shaping the way in which key aspects of life are lived.

## Culture, though, is never static.

Myriad ways of understanding what gender means reflect divergent social, cultural, political, legal, religious and economic realities worldwide. Gender roles are constructed in relation to a vast range of factors.

A

A   Traditional male labour is typical in heavy industries, such as Skinningrove blast furnace plant, which closed in 1971. In Britain, numerous steel and coal plants closed during the 1970s and 1980s under Margaret Thatcher's Conservative government.
B   These 1970s propaganda posters from the Chinese Cultural Revolution promote changing attitudes to the participation of women in the workforce. Mao Zedong wanted China's industrial strength to rival that of the West.

For example, prior to communist rule in China, a woman's role was seen in great part as domestic and decorative. By contrast, the Communist Party of China propagated the maxim 'women hold up half the sky' to make its case for gender equality to the United Nations in 2011. Life in China's major cities may have improved for women and girls – with a high percentage of girls in higher education and women in the workplace – but studies of women's experiences in rural China show continuing high rates of female illiteracy and large numbers of early arranged marriages. In other words, understandings and practices of gender are not only historically or cross-culturally wide-ranging, but also can vary greatly within the same country at the same time.

**Intersectionality** works to account for the ways in which social categories, including race, class, and gender sexuality, embodiment, and ability overlap to produce systems of oppression or disadvantage. Thus, instances of oppression in one or more of these categories should be analysed together, in context with one another.

The **United Nations** was founded in 1945 to achieve international cooperation in promoting peace, human rights and fundamental freedoms, among other matters. It currently comprises 193 member states.

In addition to linking with society's other cultural and structural factors, gender is intertwined with the system of patriarchy. The term has been developed from its original meaning by feminist writers such as Sylvia Walby (b. 1953) in *Theorizing Patriarchy* (1990) to account for social systems through which men exploit women. Writing from a sociological perspective, Walby sets out six connecting characteristics of patriarchy: 1) The state: women have less formal power and representation in government; 2) The household: women are more likely to do the housework and to raise the children; 3) Violence: women are more prone to being abused; 4) Paid work: women are likely to be paid less than men; 5) Sexuality: women's sexuality is more likely to be treated negatively; 6) Culture: women are more misrepresented in media and popular culture. Walby argues that these elements of male dominance are apparent in 'different forms in different cultures and different times'.

# In this book, we will scrutinize gender from a variety of angles, seeking to explore its different definitions and the extent to which it may be considered fluid.

A/B 'In a Parallel Universe' by Eli Rezkallah is a collection of fictional images that have been recreated from actual advertisements from the 1950s and 1960s. The series uses role play to humorously challenge contemporary sexism.

Rezkallah was prompted to create the work when he 'overheard [his] uncles talk about how women are better off cooking, taking care of the kitchen and fulfilling "their womanly duties".'

A

B

You mean a **woman** can open it?    You mean a **man** can open it?

**Patriarchy** originally referred to a society or system of government led by men, in which property was inherited through the male line and the eldest male headed the family unit. It is now used to refer to a social system in which men hold more power than women.

**Agency** is the capacity of a person or group of people to act independently or to make choices. It refers to their power to choose to act in a particular way, and to carry out their chosen action.

Chapter 1 examines how gender has been understood as a social expression of biological sex in different cultures throughout history. Chapter 2 addresses gender as a social construct and the impact of social changes on expressions of gender. Chapter 3 explores a range of practices that fall across, between or beyond the binary categories of female and male, culminating in the understanding of gender as fluid.

In addition to focusing upon gender as a social structure that may pattern inequalities and limit possibility, this book brings to light gendered agency.

Chapter 4 recognizes some of the ways in which people challenge the structures of gender. It considers how we, as individuals and as social groups, can question dominant gendered processes to create alternative ways of thinking about and living gender.

A

An **essentialist** viewpoint is based on the belief that each thing has a set of characteristics – its 'essence' – that defines it and that is fundamental to its identity and function.

**Sexual dimorphism** is the difference in characteristics – including size, colour, body structure, markings and secondary sex characteristics – between males and females of the same species, beyond those of their sexual organs.

**Sociobiologists** aim to explain social behaviours in animals and humans through a biological and evolutionary lens. They propose that, like physical traits, social behaviours have evolved in each species over time through natural selection.

# It makes sense to begin by examining the presumed relationship between gender and biological sex, as the latter is so much a part of our understandings and assumptions about the former.

What is known in gender studies as an essentialist school of thought proposes that gender differences emerge from innate disparities in the biological make-up of women and men. As well as

divergent physicalities, a biological essentialist perspective suggests that women and men possess distinct chromo-somal and hormonal variations that impact on their specific social roles – the 'essence' of masculinity and femininity.

Women, it is argued, are instinctively caring and emotionally attuned, whereas men are inherently more competent providers and protectors.

Arguing from this perspective, theorists such as Leonard Sax work on the assumption that sexual dimorphism is absolute. For them, all differences in the behaviour of women and men are biologically driven and reflect the same traits found in the animal world. Sociobiologists such as Jeremy Cherfas (b. 1951) offer a number of hypotheses along these lines. For example, they posit that men are more naturally inclined towards promiscuity because they have limitless sperm, and women are more inclined towards monogamy because – with a limited supply of eggs – they have a narrower window of opportunity to pass on their genes and must therefore pick their partner carefully. In addition, the risks and burdens of procreation, including a nine-month gestation period, potentially fatal childbirth and (arguably) the brunt of child rearing, fall to the woman. As Cherfas wrote in 2008: 'Males, with their cheap throwaway sperm, we would expect to be promiscuous; mating costs them so little they seek sexual opportunities wherever they can.'

B

A   The 'Miss America' beauty pageant was established in 1921 and is still held today. Contestants were originally judged on their looks alone, although talent and interview sections were later added. Here, a group of young beauty contestants are pictured in their evening gowns after the winner has been crowned.
B   Established in 1933, Muscle Beach in Santa Monica, California, attracted a mixed response to the overt display of physical strength. Several 'Mr Americas' trained at this beach community of weightlifters in the 1950s and 1960s.

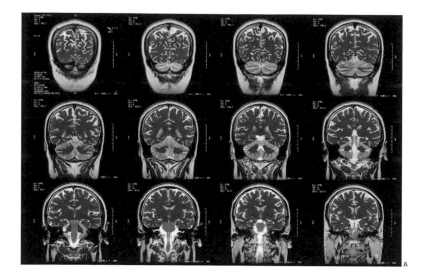

Such theories often assume that biology impacts not only on differences in sexual behaviour, but also on how women and men psychologically approach relationships. Sociobiologist Donald Symons (b. 1942) reflected this approach in 2009: 'Since human females, like those of most animal species, make a relatively large investment in the production and survival of each offspring, and males can get away with a relatively small one, they'll approach sex and reproduction, as animals do, in rather different ways to males.' Symons goes on to offer what might be termed a normative account of women's and men's approaches to sex and relationships: 'Women should be more choosy and more hesitant, because they're more at risk from the consequences of a bad choice. And men should be less discriminating, more aggressive and have a greater taste for variety of partners because they're less at risk.' Note that in this explanation, biology does not only account for what is, but also for what should be.

## In essentialist theories, the link between gendered physicality and gender-specific behaviours is often thought to be based upon hormonal and neurological differences between men and women. But not all scientists agree.

A/B These MRI scans show slices of a healthy male brain (above) and female brain (opposite). In this male brain, the cerebrum is shown in red, the cerebellum in light blue, the brainstem in green, and the tissues of the neck in brown. In this female brain, the cerebrum is shown in yellow and red, the cerebellum in pink, and the tissues of the neck in blue. Differences between male and female brains may contribute to differing characteristics and behaviours. However, opinion as to the exact effect of these differences is varied.

In *Testosterone Rex: Myths of Sex, Science and Society* (2017), psychologist and neuroscience writer Cordelia Fine challenges biological approaches that use hormonal variation.

An insistence on 'the basic and profound differences' between women and men is represented, she suggests, through the dominant story of 'Testosterone Rex', the idea that testosterone is responsible for many key social structures: 'that familiar, plausible, pervasive and powerful story of sex and society. Weaving together interlinked claims about evolution, brains, hormones and behaviour, it offers a neat and compelling account of our societies' persistent and seemingly intractable sex inequalities.' While 'Testosterone Rex can appear undefeatable', Fine argues, evolutionary theory has in fact uncovered the diversity and dynamism of the 'sexual natural order'. She cites persuasively the scientific basis for the idea that, while sex differences in hormones and brain function certainly exist, they can actually be understood to balance out the behavioural differences that arise from the physicality of different reproductive roles, rather than reinforcing them.

# So, while some physical differences between men and women serve to separate them, others work to make their behaviour more similar.

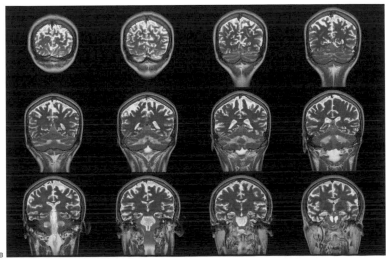

B

# Some studies in evolutionary biology and evolutionary psychology support essentialist theories of gender dimorphism.

We can examine the links between human male and female behaviour and that of animals, which, like our own, has evolved over time. Studies on animals, it is argued, show that the male is naturally inclined to be the protector or provider and the female the one to nurture. However, there are examples of animals that fall outside of this model, the Emperor penguin being the most well known. Once she lays her single egg, the female penguin goes to feed in the ocean for two months, leaving the male father to keep the egg warm by balancing it between his feet and pouch until she returns with food for their chick. The male rhea (a large, flightless species of bird) incubates the female's eggs for six weeks until they hatch. Dubbed the 'single dad' of the bird world, the male rhea is solely responsible for raising the chicks for their first six months. Some male primates also challenge preconceived ideas about sex roles in animals. The male marmoset, for example, cares for a newborn from its birth, as do the males of several rat species. Sea life offers numerous examples of 'unconventional' male reproductive behaviour. In sea horses, eggs are deposited by the female into the male's pouch, where he carries them for up to 45 days before bearing the young.

# Such examples of diversity in kin and reproductive practices in the animal world challenge the key tenets of evolutionary psychological studies that insist on natural sex and gender

A

A    A male emu nests with its eggs. The male of this species is responsible for incubating and nurturing the young.
B    A male Emperor penguin looks after its chick. Once she lays her egg, the female penguin leaves the nest to spend the winter in the ocean. The male penguin hatches the egg and nurtures the young.
C    During the mating process, the female sea horse deposits eggs in a pouch on the male's tail. He then carries the eggs until they hatch.

B

C

**Evolutionary biology** is the study of evolutionary processes in nature, such as natural selection, common descent and the ways in which life forms have diversified and adapted over time.

**Evolutionary psychology** proposes that some or all human behaviour is based on psychological adaptations that, like physical traits, developed as a response to environmental pressures as humans evolved.

**Kin and reproductive practices** are, respectively, the ways in which organisms interact with their relatives and the ways in which they reproduce. Both sets of practices may differ greatly between species.

difference. In the human world, too, it is increasingly common for men to participate in some or all of the childcare, or for women to take on the role of provider.

Other modern ways of living intimate and sexual lives cannot be accounted for in theories of sexual dimorphism. Terms such as 'voluntarily childless' or 'childfree' have been coined to describe the increasing numbers of women and men who are choosing not to have children in the 21st century. The most recent statistics from the US Census Bureau's 'Current Population Survey' (2014) reported that almost half of women between the ages of 15 and 44 do not have children, a figure higher than at any other time since the government began demographic tracking of reproduction.

This Golden Dreams pin-up calendar from 1955 features US actress Marilyn Monroe posing nude. The original shot was taken by photographer Tom Kelley in 1949 when Monroe was desperate for money. She was paid $50.

In 1999, members of the Rylstone and District Women's Institute modelled naked for a charity calendar. They became internationally famous when the film *Calendar Girls* (2003) told their story. Here, new members join some of the originals and rename themselves the 'Baker's Half Dozen'.

# Uncoupling sex and reproduction challenges the analysis of sex as an innate and universal practice.

## Sociobiological theories of the gendered nature of sexual behaviour, such as promiscuity and monogamy, are also questionable in light of current findings.

A recent survey on sexual health by the health and beauty company Superdrug, for example, questioned 2,000 men and women in Britain and Europe about their sexual lifestyles. The number of sexual partners reported by women (14) was almost equivalent to the figure given by men (15), and women were just as likely as men to have affairs. Sexual research thus upends the binary myth of the naturally promiscuous man and the monogamous woman.

In *The Human Journey* (2012), historian Kevin Reilly points out that archaeological evidence suggests ancient societies, such as pre-Neolithic hunter-gatherers, often divided labour according to sex: 'In most cases, men hunted, usually in small groups, while women gathered plants and small animals with the children, closer to home.'

A common approach based on evolutionary psychology envisages sex roles in the modern world as following the same 'naturally prescribed' pattern of men hunting while women forage and care for children.

It is argued that each sex is best suited to their allotted role because they have evolved the optimal characteristics for carrying it out: for example, men's upper body strength (on average greater than women's) and high levels of testosterone (increasing the tendency for aggression and risk-taking) might be said to make them better suited for hunting.

B

Baker's half dozen . . .

A

Anthropologists Steven L. Kuhn and Mary C. Stiner hypothesize in their article 'What's a Mother to Do?' (2006) that this division of labour during the Palaeolithic era gave *Homo sapiens* an advantage over Neanderthals by allowing them to expand their diet and cooperate to increase efficiency. However, they stress that '...the universal tendency to divide subsistence labour by gender is not solely the result of innate physical or psychological differences between the sexes; much of it has to be learned.'

It is important to note also that anthropological studies into the hunter-gatherer societies that still exist suggest that women in these communities hunt alongside men.

The Aeta people of the Philippines are one such society. Similarly, female members of both the hunter-gatherer community Ju/'hoansi in Namibia and the Australian hunter-gatherer Martu community are proficient hunters.

B

A   Women of the
    Aka people in the
    Central African
    Republic head
    to the forest for
    a day's fishing.
    Aka fathers play
    an equal part
    in childcare,
    spending 47% of
    their time within
    reach of their
    children.

B   The Aeta are
    an indigenous
    people who live
    in mountainous
    parts of the island
    of Luzon
    in the Philippines.
    According to
    one study, women
    hunters have a
    higher success
    rate than men.

In *Man the Hunter* (1968), anthropologists Richard Borshay Lee and Irven DeVore suggest that egalitarianism is a key characteristic of nomadic hunting and gathering societies. Because this lifestyle requires group members to be mobile, material possessions must be distributed throughout the group, so one individual cannot accumulate a surplus. A further study in 2015 by anthropologist Mark Dyble proposes that sexual equality was evolutionarily advantageous in early human societies because it fostered wide-ranging social networks. Dyble suggests that sexual inequalities first appeared following the development of agriculture, as communities settled in fixed locations and resources could be accumulated. At this point in human history, Dyble says, it began to be advantageous for men to amass resources – including wives and children – and to form alliances with male kin.

Dyble's interpretation is among those proposing that differing social roles for men and women came about as a result of changing social factors, rather than biological evolution – a theory that will be explored in more depth in Chapter 2.

# Whether or not the biological make-up of women and men impacted on gendered behaviours and social roles, it was imperfectly understood for a great proportion of human history.

Sexual historian Thomas Laqueur (b. 1945) argues that the foundations were laid for modern understandings of human sex and sexuality in Europe in the 18th century, during the period

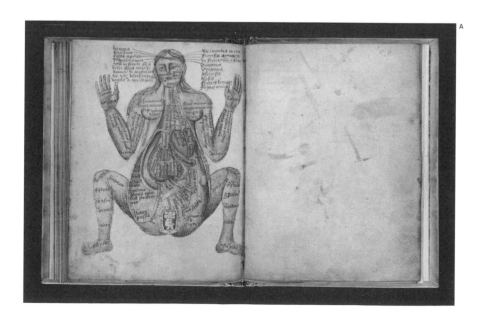

A

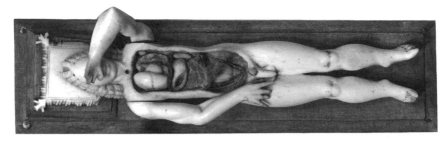

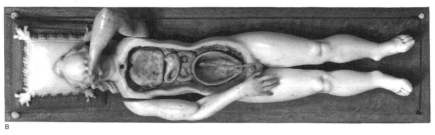

B

known as the **Enlightenment**. During this time, science took over from religion as the dominant explanatory framework for sex and gender difference.

Laqueur defines this shift as signifying a move from a 'one-sex' to a 'two-sex' model in late 18th-century Western Europe. Previously, Laqueur suggests, the prevailing belief – a tradition that dated back at least to ancient Greece – was that women and men represented 'one sex'. Men and women were characterized as possessing variations in one type of human body, whereby male genitalia were on the body's outside and female genitalia were something like a mirror image of the same anatomy, on the inside.

The **Enlightenment** is a historical period stretching from the late 17th to early 19th centuries, during which European science, philosophy and politics underwent radical changes, emphasizing science, reason and individualism over religion and tradition.

A  'Pregnant Woman', from the 15th-century English medical treatise *Anatomia* attributed to Pseudo-Galen.
B  Male and female anatomical figures made from ivory (1701–30). The organs are not depicted in great detail, so it is unlikely that the figures were used for medical teaching.

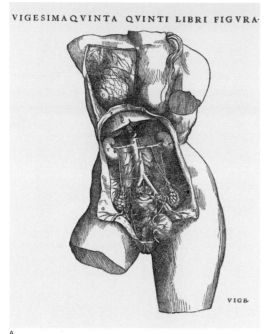

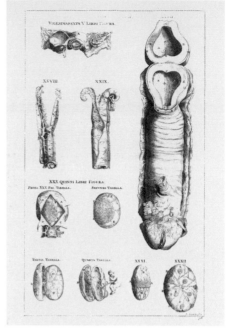

A Andreas Vesalius was the foremost pioneer of modern anatomy. These illustrations are from his best-known work *De Humani Corporis Fabrica* (On the Fabric of the Human Body, 1543), depicting the female anatomy (left) and the vaginal canal resembling an inverted penis (right).

B A male skeleton with a horse (left) and a female skeleton with an ostrich (right). From a series of engravings by Edward Mitchell that appear in *The Anatomy of the Bones of the Human Body* (1829) by John Barclay.

The **gender binary** system classifies gender into two categories: male and female. It takes these categories to be discrete and opposite to one another. This system sometimes conflates the biological and social aspects of gender.

The belief that the female body therefore represented an inferior or imperfect version of the male was supported by the studies of men such as Galen, a Greek physician living in the Roman Empire, and Andreas Vesalius, a 16th-century Flemish anatomist who was an early and influential part of the movement for the use of dissection in discovering the realities of the human body.

From Vesalius's time, and onwards into the 18th-century Enlightenment, marked changes occurred in how human sex was viewed. Scientific advances, achieved through practices such as dissection, revealed physical differences between men and women far beyond their reproductive systems. According to science historian Londa Schiebinger (b. 1952) in 'Skeletons in the Closet' (1986): 'Beginning in the 1750s, doctors in France and Germany called for a finer delineation of sex differences; discovering, describing and defining sex differences in every bone, muscle, nerve and vein became a research priority in anatomical science.' Rather than the female body being an imperfect, inverted version of the male body, a gender binary model emphasized the two as being more deeply different.

Laqueur describes this as the emergence of the two-sex model. He and Schiebinger both cite changing depictions of the human skeleton in Western European medical textbooks during this period; previously, there had been one depiction of a human skeleton in medical illustration – a male skeleton, as the one-sex model might suggest.

As ideas stressing difference became more dominant, depictions of the singular human skeleton were replaced by drawings of two quite different skeletal figures – one of a woman and one of a man.

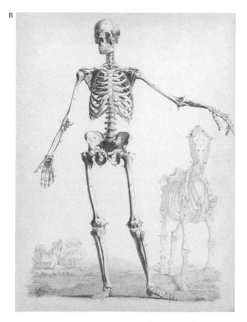
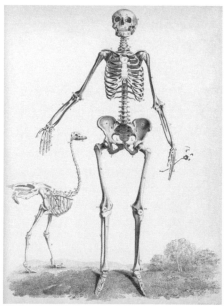

B

A

As difference became the focus of enquiry, scientists sought to identify the 'source' of what made a woman and what made a man. Scientific, philosophical and political discourse during the Enlightenment often focused on the case for individual freedom and equality for all people. Questions arose about whether women should be included in this demand for equality. In his *Lettres persanes* of 1721, Montesquieu notes: 'It is a great question, among men, to know whether it is more advantageous to deprive women of liberty than to leave it to them; it seems to me that there are many reasons for and against.' He raises the question of 'whether natural law submits women to men'.

The fact that science stressed the differences between men and women at this time, when huge developments in political and ethical philosophy were under way concerning individual rights, was perhaps advantageous to those looking to justify women's subordinate role in society. Certainly, the fact that the female skull is typically smaller than the male skull – indicating a correspondingly smaller brain – was used during the 19th century as an argument that women were less capable of rational thought than men.

A   Although untitled, this oil painting by Joseph Wright of Derby is known as 'A Philosopher Giving that Lecture on the Orrery, in which a Lamp Is Put in Place of the Sun' or, more simply, 'The Orrery' (c. 1766). The painting resembles a conversation piece, but its scientific subject matter was a break with tradition. During the Enlightenment, science and rationality were often linked with masculinity.

B   *First Steps*, or *The Nourishing Mother* (1803–04) by Marguerite Gérard portrays the themes of maternal tenderness and maternity, for which the artist was best known. Historically, women have often been associated with nurturing behaviour.

B

With the development of a two-sex model, Laqueur says, men and women's social roles came to be seen as distinct within scientific thought, as they had been before within the social and religious framework.

As science developed its ideas of gender as binary, biology was used to justify men's association with rationality and culture, and women's with emotion and nature.

A

B

In 18th-century discourse, women's bodies defined their nature as maternal and nurturing. Changing understandings of gender had deep social repercussions, giving scientific support to ideas that had existed before as religious, cultural or philosophical beliefs. Influential philosophers such as Jean-Jacques Rousseau (1712–78) proposed that men were more suited to public roles, while women were connected to the private realm and naturally took on a more subservient role. Public roles acquired higher status during the Enlightenment, so that men gained greater levels of power in society through changing understandings of the sexed body.

We should note, however, that there were women who challenged their exclusion from public life during this time. For example, many upper- and middle-class women took part in intellectual salons, discussing literature, politics and philosophy alongside men. Female authors, particularly of the novel, began to emerge during the Enlightenment, and in 1792 Mary Wollstonecraft (1759–97) wrote *A Vindication of the Rights of Woman: With Strictures on Political and Moral Subjects*, which critiqued the male theorists who argued against the education of women. However, for many women, and for working-class women especially, dominant understandings of gendered difference constrained them to the domestic sphere.

# These power disparities have been hard to break down.

The stress placed by the two-sex model on the biological differences between women and men is still evident in many understandings of gender today; such differences are emphasized by and linked to natural phenomena. However, another important flaw in traditional biological perspectives is that they do not account for people whose biological sex seems to fall between or outside of the categories of man or woman.

The work of biologist Anne Fausto-Sterling marks a radical departure from established ways of theorizing gender and biology. Fausto-Sterling argues that a gender-binary understanding of the existence of only two biological sexes is deeply problematic. This, she suggests in *Sexing the Body* (2000), is an incorrect reading of biology that has come to be interpreted as a truth in modern society: in reality, 'complete maleness and complete femaleness represent the extreme ends of a spectrum of possible body types'. Within the opposites of male and female lie a multitude of variations. Biological sex can be construed as a spectrum, with the majority of people clustered towards 'male' or 'female', but with a small – but nonetheless significant – spread of other possibilities in between. Chromosomal variations in gender are vast and differ much further than XX and XY. There are, for example, many different intersex conditions, and so, even within sex and gender variations, there is diversity.

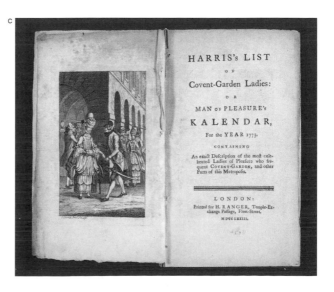

A   *Chevalier d'Eon* (1792) by Thomas Stewart, after Jean Laurent Mosnier. The chevalier lived as a man from 1762 to 1777 and as a woman from 1786 to 1810. Here, the sitter wears a black fencing dress.

B   In *Mary Wollstonecraft* (c. 1797) by John Opie, the sitter is plainly dressed and has a simple hairstyle. This reflects Wollstonecraft's views on dress: that is should 'adorn the person and not rival it'.

C   An edition of *Harris's List of Covent Garden Ladies* (1773). Produced for clients, the publication was an annual directory of women selling sex in Georgian London.

HARRIS's LIST
OF
Covent-Garden Ladies:
OR
MAN of PLEASURE's
KALENDAR,
For the YEAR 1773.
CONTAINING
An exact Description of the most celebrated Ladies of Pleasure who frequent COVENT-GARDEN, and other Parts of this Metropolis.

LONDON:
Printed for H. RANGER, Temple-Exchange Passage, Fleet-Street,
MDCCLXXIII.

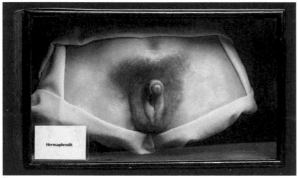

A

**Intersex** (DSD) describes various conditions in which a person has reproductive or sexual anatomy that does not fit typical definitions of male or female. DSD (disorders/differences/diversities of sexual development) io the term currently used by the medical establishment to describe such conditions, although some people diagnosed with DSD prefer to describe themselves as intersex.

**Transgender** is an umbrella term describing people whose innate gender identity or gender expression is different to the sex they were assigned at birth. Some transgender people decide to transition from one biological sex to another; these people are sometimes referred to as transsexual. Others prefer not to transition physically.

**Cisgender** people experience their gender identity, gender expression and biological sex as consistent with each other. The word also implies a person who performs the gender role that social convention dictates is appropriate to their sex. It is sometimes abbreviated to 'cis'.

Tongue in cheek, Fausto-Sterling proposes a five- not a two-sex model, including male, female, merm, ferm and herm (abbreviation of hermaphrodite).

Work on intersex shows that gender development is far more varied than a two-sex model admits. It is hard to ascertain the numbers of babies born intersex, as medical advice has led traditionally to surgical 'correction' at birth, so that the child develops as either a boy or a girl. The Intersex Campaign for Equality notes that 'the most thorough existing research' estimates that intersex people make up around 1.7% to 2% of the population. This is about the same as the percentage of people who are born with red hair (1% to 2%).

There has been great stigma around intersex conditions, and sometimes children are not told that they have had corrective surgery. Enabled by the Internet, intersex communities have formed in recent years and activism against surgical intervention on babies is growing, particularly in North America. Such surgeries, activists argue, are unethical: they are carried out without the child's consent and may lead to serious medical and psychological problems in later life.

Despite the existence of people with intersex variations and transgender people (see Chapters 2 and 3), it is possible – indeed, likely – for gender identity to be aligned with biological sex. Many humans experience this alignment, which is commonly known as being cisgender. A binary biological approach assuming the existence of this alignment is still taken in much scientific research and sociobiology.

A   These wax models of genitals were displayed in 1873 at Caston's Panopticon in Berlin, alongside models showing the effects of different venereal diseases. Nowadays, there is controversy over the pathologization of intersex conditions.

B   Two from a series of nine photographs, taken by Nadar in 1860, showing a person with an intersex condition. They were not published, but used for scientific research and teaching.

A

B

Proponents of this approach use biological arguments centred around differences in brain structure and hormonal levels to explain differences in gender behaviour, experience or social roles. The theory that these differences are innate and are visible in scans of the brain has gained widespread popularity through best-selling books such as John Gray's *Men Are from Mars, Women Are from Venus* (2002). Gray argues, for example, that men's natural superiority of spatial skill means that they have greater ability to park a car or to map-read, whereas women have superior skill when it comes to emotional or linguistic intelligence.

These distinct abilities are, according to Gray and many others, 'hard-wired' in the brain, and are reflected in the gender roles that men and women naturally choose to assume.

Despite this, some scientists are increasingly challenging the model of gender that focuses on differentiation. Instead, they point to the similarities between women and men. In particular, a number are rejecting what they term

C

D

## 'neurosexism' and are challenging the idea that men and women are neurologically different.

In her book *Delusions of Gender* (2010), Cordelia Fine argues that the brain in both men and women is 'flexible, malleable and changeable'. Lise Eliot, a medical academic, also disputes the notion that men and women are 'made' differently, arguing in 2010 that 'there is almost nothing we do with our brains that is hard-wired. Every skill, attribute and personality trait is moulded by experience.' In this model, human physiology is both the cause of behaviours *and* is affected by them; our experiences 'wire' our brain, which feeds back into how we experience things.

A  French writer and actress Colette had relationships with both men and women (including the Marquise de Belbeuf, who dressed as a man). She wrote extensively about female sexuality and gender roles.

B  British novelist and poet Radclyffe Hall often dressed in masculine clothing, and was known to friends as 'John'.

C  British model, actor and writer Quentin Crisp, who was known for his effeminate appearance and behaviour, was one of a small number of gay men who were 'out' in London in the 1930s and 1940s.

D  Self-portrait by US pop artist Andy Warhol. His work often explored themes of gender, sexuality and desire.

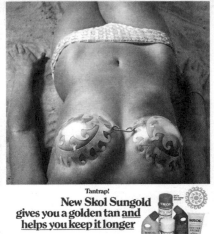

**Nurturance** is the providing of emotional and physical care to another person, meeting their need for such care. A social behaviour present in humans and many animals, it is often constructed as 'feminine', but in fact can be displayed by people of all genders.

**Ethnomethodology** is the study of the ways in which people make sense of their world and create the social environment in which they live. It views people as rational actors who employ pragmatic reasoning to enable them to function in society.

Fine points to a 2012 study by Sari van Anders concerning childcare. Women tend to have lower base levels of testosterone than men, and since lower testosterone levels are linked to nurturance, we might infer that this makes women biologically better suited to childcare than men. In the van Anders study, three groups of men were asked to care for a programmable model baby. One group was told to sit and listen to the baby crying (playing the 'traditional male' role of leaving childcare to someone else); another group was instructed to interact with the baby, but the baby was programmed to cry no matter what they did (mimicking someone inexperienced with childcare); the final group was also told to interact with the baby, but the baby was programmed to be consolable when comforted in the correct way (replicating the role of someone more experienced with childcare). Their testosterone levels were measured throughout. In the first two groups, testosterone levels rose as the situation unfolded, but in the last group – the one simulating nurturance – testosterone levels fell when the baby was comforted. So while lower testosterone levels might be linked to nurturance, successful nurturance might also *create* lower testosterone levels.

This cycle of cause and effect makes it difficult to disentangle the biological causes of gendered behaviour from the social or experiential ones.

An understanding that men and women each possess characteristics considered to be both masculine and feminine was central to sociological, and some psychological, studies of gender identity from the 1970s.

The field of ethnomethodology examined how gender was located in social interaction and everyday activity. Rather than being a universal experience, gender was seen as rooted in the 'things that we do'. In their article titled 'Doing Gender' (1987), Candace West and Don H. Zimmerman examined how gender was performed through social interactions. Gender, they argued, was 'omni-relevant'. The need to 'do' gender correctly in relation to society's expectations of what is appropriate gendered behaviour weighs heavily in all activities, however much we take them for granted. Failure to perform gender correctly carries the social stigma of being considered un-masculine or un-feminine.

A   These 1970s sunscreen adverts treat the female body as an object and imply that appearance is paramount for women. Advertisers often use gendered stereotypes to sell products; the pressure to perform gender correctly can powerfully motivate consumers.
B   This advert for *Max Power* car magazine positions the man as owner and the woman as possession, framing both her and the car as 'accessories'.

B

Accessories to be seen with

Max Cars. Max Babes. *Max Power Magazine*.
On sale 15th of every month.

A

In *Gender Trouble* (1990), gender studies scholar and philosopher Judith Butler (b. 1956) further separated biological sex from gender: 'When the constructed status of gender is theorized as radically independent of sex, gender itself becomes a free-floating artifice, with the consequence that *man* and *masculine* might just as easily signify a female body as a male one, and *woman* and *feminine* a male body as easily as a female one.'

This enabled a broader understanding of ways of living gender, taking account of, for example, the masculine woman or the feminine man. The work of Jack Halberstam on female masculinity in 1999, for example, shows that having what is considered to be a female body does not necessarily result in expressions of femininity, or the identity of 'woman'. Mimi Schippers's 2007 study of male femininity indicates that, vice versa, being identified as male at birth does not necessarily lead to the behaviour or expressions that are considered typically masculine.

B

# These studies present a distinct challenge to the reduction of gender to biological difference.

A   This photograph of 'Chris' appeared in *My Comrade* magazine in 1989. It was taken by drag queen Linda Simpson as part of her historical photo essay *Every Night in Drag*, which documented New York City's drag scene from the late 1980s to the mid 1990s.

B   'Tabboo! at Joe's Pub' (1995) is from the same series, which comprised over 5,000 photographs. Drag challenges the assumption that male bodies cannot be feminine, or female bodies masculine.

Biology clearly does not represent the sum of gender; not only is it undetermined how far our gendered bodies contribute to our behaviour, but not all bodies *are* biologically male or female – they are both, or neither.

# 2. Gender as a Social Construct

A

# Opinions vary on how far biology contributes to gendered experiences and behaviour.

A social constructionist view of gender proposes that gender roles – the patterns of behaviour prescribed as 'normal' or 'ideal' for each sex – are not entirely determined by human biology and evolution, but are to some degree created and perpetuated for each sex by the society and culture we live in. Gender identities and expressions that fall outside this prescribed behaviour are presented as 'abnormal'.

To evaluate this, we can examine how gender roles have been perceived historically by different societies and cultures, and how they are dealt with across the world today.

A   Today, gendered social pressures are sometimes perpetuated by advertising. This advert for weight loss products by Protein World encourages women's bodily anxieties by suggesting that only slim women are 'ready' to wear a bikini.

B   Recently, more advertisers have begun to mock or subvert traditional gender roles. These print adverts created for Nanny by Thai advertising agency Monday in 2012 depict male nannies feeding babies using breast milk storage bags.

Historians such as Joan Wallach Scott (b. 1941), Sheila Rowbotham (b. 1943) and Hilary Wainwright (b. 1949) critique the biological perspective by suggesting that approaching gender through a historical lens reveals more complex findings, with changing understandings and expectations about gender emerging over time.

The earliest human societies were bands of nomadic hunter-gatherers, but in some regions, from around 10,000 years ago, people began to settle in one place and to grow their own food, giving rise to the agrarian social model. Since productive farms can feed more people than are required to run the farm itself, these societies developed food surpluses, enabling some people to engage in activities not directly related to feeding themselves, such as military conquest, developing advanced technology and engaging in trade.

A **social constructionist** view maintains that humans actively construct their social world through their interactions and shared assumptions. This sociological theory suggests that human understandings of social reality are created jointly, rather than stemming from a natural external 'truth'.

An **agrarian** society is one whose economy is focused primarily on agriculture, cultivating crops and raising livestock in large fields. The majority of societies existing after the hunter-gatherer period of human development were agrarian, until industrialization occurred in the 18th and 19th centuries.

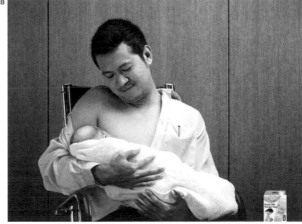

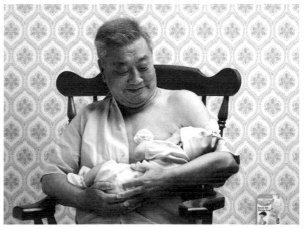

In such societies, land ownership or control was the main source of wealth and status, and later this attitude was extended to ownership and control in general. Property, not labour, was a source of social status – and property was most often owned or managed by the highest status male of a family group.

Early agrarian societies were based around a family or communal unit, with each person having a distinct role in food production. A common division of labour in these societies was that men carried out work in the fields, while women undertook management of the house, prepared food, spun wool or produced clothing, and cared for children and dependents. This division may have been based around factors such as male upper body strength – on average greater – or the female reproductive role, which meant that without birth control fertile women might frequently be pregnant or breastfeeding and thus to some degree unavailable for work in the fields. It was difficult or impossible for an individual to support him- or herself outside the family or communal unit. It made sense, therefore, for assets to belong to the family unit rather than to the individual, and because a man almost always headed the family unit, he most often accumulated, managed and protected those assets.

As agrarian societies grew more advanced – developing into the civilizations of ancient Egypt, Greece and Rome, among others – the gender

A

A   This Late Period Egyptian fragment of a relief depicts the preparation of lily essence by women. The flowers are pressed in a cloth made of linen and then twisted.

B   This New Kingdom Egyptian fragment of a wall painting depicts men sowing and harvesting. Women also appear, at the left hand side of the central row. The fragment is from the tomb of Onsu at west Thebes.

B

roles from early agrarian cultures were enshrined in religious and cultural norms, even after the circumstances that created them had changed.

In all three of the aforementioned civilizations, the female sphere of influence was broadly considered to be domestic, while the male sphere extended to public life. The head of a household was the highest status man.

In some agrarian societies, such as ancient Greece, the tendency for men to own or manage the assets of the family unit developed to the point where women were not allowed to own property at all, or to buy anything more expensive than a *medimnos* (bushel) of barley. Although ancient Greece is known as the birthplace of democracy, Greek women were not allowed to vote, and many were required to be under the control and protection of a *kyrios* (male guardian) at all times.

A

Situations like this subordinated women to men, forcing them to rely on male asset-owners for food, protection and support. This was understood to be natural, as in Aristotle's pronouncement that 'between the sexes, the male is by nature superior and the female inferior, the male ruler and the female subject'.

Property in agrarian societies was usually passed down through the generations, so a person's status depended on their lineage. Restricting female sexuality was a way of policing this: the mother of a child could be clearly identified, while the father could not. Female chastity (before marriage) and fidelity (during marriage) were important in order to guarantee that both parents of a child could be identified, cementing its social status and right to inherit.

Despite their fundamental similarities in assigning women to the domestic sphere and men to the public sphere, there are some interesting differences between these societies, too. For example, in ancient Egypt, women had equal rights and responsibilities to men in the eyes of the law. They were able to own and inherit property, initiate divorce, enter into a contract, make a will and borrow money.

A   Greek Attic red-figure vase paintings from c. 480–500 BC, showing intimate details of women's lives. (Left to Right): At the laver; in the women's quarters; *hetaera* dancing and *hetaera* urinating. *Hetaerae* were often independent courtesans (unlike *pornai*, slaves used as prostitutes).

# In many advanced agrarian societies, including ancient Greece and Rome, it was a sign of status for a woman not to work.

It implied that her husband or father had the resources to support her, which increased his status and that of the family unit. However, in practice, even the highest status women were usually expected to manage a household of servants or slaves, who carried out the manual labour necessary to maintain the home and care for children.

Women from poorer backgrounds or women without a male guardian to support them had to work for a living, as did slaves. Prostitution was one option. Others included working with a family on a smallholding; spinning, weaving or making clothing; caring for another woman's children; working as a midwife; housekeeping or cleaning; or acting as a priestess, most often in a sect worshipping a deity personified as female. Different professions predominated in different societies, but not all women were supported by male family members. Consequently, some women had to work outside the home to look after themselves, to contribute to their family's income, or because they were enslaved.

Agrarian societies and their attitudes to gender persisted until the Industrial Revolution, which in Europe began in the late 18th century and continued throughout the 19th century. Before this, the majority of people in Europe lived in small rural communities. Women often participated in vital cottage industries such as spinning. At harvest time, women, men and children laboured together to collect crops. In urban areas, women worked alongside men in trades and crafts, creating textiles, and leather and metal products.

A

The **Meiji period** in Japan was the era during which the country began to transition from an isolated feudal society to its more outward-looking modern incarnation. This occurred under the leadership of the emperor, who had been 'restored' to power following the defeat of the Tokugawa shogun and his government, the new de facto political leaders.

A   This Roman mosaic from the 4th-century Villa Romana del Casale in Sicily depicts girls in bikinis playing sport. The girl in the toga presents a crown and frond to the victor.
B   The Codex Mendoza (*c.* 1542) portrays the various training of Aztec boys and girls from the age of seven to ten. For example, (top) the boy is being taught to fish and the girl is learning to twirl a spindle. Punishments are also specified (third row), in which the boy is pierced and bound and the girl has her wrists pricked.

B

Rather than representing scientific progress or advanced medical understandings, the development of the two-sex model during the 17th and 18th centuries can be understood through economic and political shifts, particularly concerning women's ability to work alongside or in competition with men.

Indeed, throughout the world, the evolving understanding of gender difference in the modern age can be mapped onto each region's changing economic needs, brought about by their respective industrial revolutions. In Japan, for example, the Industrial Revolution occurred later than in the West, beginning in around 1870 during the Meiji period, and created a role change for women similar to that in the West.

During the first part of the Industrial Revolution in the West, women and children worked alongside men in the developing industries (although campaigns against child labour saw both children's and women's hours decreasing and, eventually, disappearing again).

# Although working-class women had always had to find work, during the Industrial Revolution the nature of this work changed.

New technologies in industries such as textiles, pottery, mass-produced food and clothing displaced the skilled men who had dominated them. Women and children – willing to work for less and initially, perhaps, less resentful of new methods – began to replace men or to supplement their numbers. Trade unions, acting in the interests of their male members, opposed the idea of women taking up the traditionally masculine role of breadwinner.

A

A   This plate from 'The Linen Manufactory of Ireland' (1791) shows methods of preparing flax used in the 18th century, when many women worked in cottage industries such as spinning.

B   Female workers labour in the cotton doubling room at Dean Mills, Manchester, in 1851. Women were often employed in textile factories during the early stages of the Industrial Revolution.

As occasional, subordinate members of the workforce, women had not been a threat, but now – at least in some industries – they were undercutting men. Leaders of some religions, including the dominant Christianity, were also concerned that the feminine gender role appeared to be in flux, contradicting the teachings of many religious texts.

If it could be maintained, the age-old social construction of ideal femininity, wherein the woman stayed at home and cared for her husband and children, was a solution to these fears.

A  This fashion plate is from the July 1875 edition of *Godey's Lady's Book*. The publication was the most popular US women's magazine before the Civil War (1830–78). The plate depicts the corseted, full-skirted dresses fashionable for upper-class women at the time.

B  US exhibition shooter and renowned markswoman Annie Oakley, born Phoebe Ann Mosey, had a starring role in Buffalo Bill's Wild West show.

C  US frontierswoman and scout Calamity Jane, born Martha Jane Canary, became infamous for her claim that she fought Indians alongside Wild Bill Hickok.

Both religious leaders and trade unions had a significant influence on society. The working woman (and hence the working-class woman) was presented in dominant gendered discourse as a failing woman. The middle-class ideal of the man as provider and the woman as carer, which might have been entirely displaced by the Industrial Revolution, instead remained firmly entrenched into the 19th and early 20th centuries.

Marxist feminist writers such as Christine Delphy (b. 1941) argue that this model suited capitalism: women provided unpaid domestic labour, a 'reserve army' of cheap commercial labour, and a means for producing and socializing the next generation of workers. It was justified as reflecting an 'ideal' natural order, backed up by the science of the day with the 'two-sex' model. This ideal has been very hard to dispel, although it was untenable for those who needed a woman's wages to support the household.

**Discourse** refers in general to all spoken and written communication, but can be used more specifically to mean formal discussion – especially academic discussion – of a particular topic. Within the social sciences and humanities, discourse accounts for dominant ways of thinking about a particular topic.

**Capitalism** is an economic and political system in which trade and industry are controlled by private owners for profit.

Notable exceptions to the ideal also existed, in 'frontier' cultures such as those of New Zealand and the American West. There, colonizing women necessarily took on roles traditionally framed as masculine – such as shooting, driving teams of horses, and protecting and providing for their families – when their fathers, husbands or brothers were away or incapacitated. Correspondingly, New Zealand and some western states of the USA were among the first to grant women the right to vote (although the USA as a whole did not do so until 1920) and in some cases to inherit property.

In Britain, meanwhile, the conflict between notions of ideal femininity and the increasing number of women workers became a source of concern for the Victorian middle classes. Domestic service and care work were seen as the answer, and were promoted as good forms of training for marriage.

MISS ANNIE OAKLEY
(LITTLE SURE SHOT)
CABINET PORTRAIT

Calamity Jane Gen Custers
Finn Livingston Mont.

A

To educate working-class women was to civilize them through the fostering of domestic duties, which was a means of instilling middle-class domestic standards, as illustrated in a Government Report from 1904:

> 'At 13 years of age the majority of these women would have begun to work in a factory, to handle their own earning, to mix with large numbers of people with all the excitement and gossip of factory life. They would in this case grow up entirely ignorant of everything pertaining to domesticity...Until girls have been taught to find pleasure in domestic work it is useless to expect them to relinquish factory life.'

A similar backlash against the changing role of women is reflected in Japan's Meiji Civil Code, enacted in 1898, around 30 years after the beginning of the country's Industrial Revolution, which required that a wife obtain the permission of her husband for: 'Receiving or employing capital; contracting a loan or giving security; doing any act whose object is the acquiring or parting with a right in an immovable or a valuable movable; doing any act in the course of a lawsuit; making a gift, a compromise, or an agreement to submit to arbitration; accepting or refusing a succession; accepting or refusing a gift or a legacy; making any contract affecting the disposition of her person.'

In *Formations of Class and Gender: Becoming Respectable* (1997), gender studies scholar Beverley Skeggs argues that the notion of 'respectability' remains as central to the constructions of gender today as it did in the 19th century. To be a 'good woman' is often equated with being a respectable woman, displaying restraint, control and a lack of 'excess', qualities that mirror middle-class cultural values of good taste.

# Historically, as well as in contemporary society, morals are key to the construction of femininity.

Alongside cultural values and legal rights, religion is also significant in setting up and maintaining gendered moral codes and gender roles. Religious moral codes stressing women's purity and emphasizing the importance of female chasteness legitimize sex segregation in public life and religious practice.

Many key religious texts convey the gender roles traditional to ancient agrarian societies, presenting these behavioural patterns as necessary to live correctly and achieve salvation after death.

The separation of women and men within strands of Judaism, Islam and Christianity seeks to protect female purity against the perceived uncontrollable nature of male sexuality. These ideas are apparent in wider discourses around gender and sexuality in contemporary society, where women are frequently held accountable for sexual harassment and violence through, for example, their choice of clothing or alcohol consumption. Similarly, modern-day conservative religious communities such as the Amish or Orthodox Jews choose to adhere closely to traditional male and female gender roles in both public and private life.

By contrast, Chinese accounts of ancient Japanese society, dating from around the 1st century BC, claim that in Japan at that time there was no social distinction between men and women, and that there were female rulers. While the historical context of these accounts makes it possible that they were intended to denigrate the Japanese, such egalitarian behaviour could be explained by the Shinto religion, practised in Japan at that time. Early Shintoism is thought to have included the worship of Amaterasu, the creator and sun goddess, leading to a matriarchal religion in which feminine qualities were embraced and admired in balance with masculine ones.

A

A   *Origin of Music and Dance at the Rock Door* (1887) by Shunsai Toshimasa depicts Amaterasu, the Japanese sun goddess, emerging from a cave.

B   This photograph depicts a zenana carriage from the 1880s, used to transport women. All sides of the carriage are covered to protect the woman's modesty and to uphold the seclusion demanded by purdah.

The **Shinto** religion is the indigenous faith of Japan. It is still Japan's major religion along with Buddhism. Its early forms were clearly distinguished from Buddhism, but it took on some Buddhist and Confucian traits over time.

**Purdah** is a form of female seclusion in some Hindu and Muslim communities in South Asia. Women who practise purdah are screened from view, particularly male view, by means of clothing (including the veil) and segregation behind walls, screens or curtains.

B

# Changing economic conditions and policies may contradict religious understandings of gender.

Shifts in economic and political systems have remained a key influencing factor in gendered experiences. In Bangladesh, for example, changes in trade policies beginning in the late 1970s enabled the development of the garment industry, which needed a new influx of workers into the labour market. These workers came from the large numbers of women who moved to urban areas in search of work, a phenomenon at variance with the traditional values of purdah, which separate women from men in public and demand that they cover their bodies and faces. The process of women entering the workforce in cities has led to a more relaxed view of purdah in urban areas and within families who need the wage of the woman. By turn, this feeds into broader public perceptions of possibilities for women in society.

A

A historical consideration of purdah, however, shows that factors such as caste and class always impacted upon cultural values, with families of lower castes and classes needing the wages of women, who worked alongside men in fields. Only wealthy families, who did not need women to work, performed purdah strictly.

Another example of changing conditions contradicting gendered religious practices is the way in which the traditional Hindu practice of sati has been understood in the West. Women who perform sati burn themselves on their husband's funeral pyre. While this has historically been understood as an act of honour within Hindu thinking, from a liberal and particularly a feminist Western perspective, it symbolizes coercion and violence against women.

In 1829 sati was outlawed by British colonial powers in India. What we have known about sati has always come, says writer Gayatri Spivak in her essay 'Can the Subaltern Speak?' (1988), from British colonizers, never from the women involved themselves. Her statement 'White men are saving brown women from brown men' complicates the questions of power. The central question of debate here is a common one: is it patriarchal custom or the individual women's autonomy that enable this practice? Or is it a mixture of both? Spivak and other post-colonial feminists would argue the latter.

As in the example of purdah, when countries are invaded or colonized gendered roles and expectations from the colonizing nation can be introduced and can develop alongside local understandings of gender. Gendered expectations may clash and be experienced in complex or contradictory ways.

In parts of South America, for example, Spanish rule has influenced the demarcation of gendered roles within the family. Indigenous gender models and the modern demands of capitalism, both of which deem women an important part of the workforce, exist alongside these family roles. Conflicting expectations, created on the one hand by the labour market and on the other by family duty, present incompatible responsibilities for women here, as in many parts of the world.

**Sati** was a Hindu funeral custom in which a widow self-immolated on her husband's pyre; it is no longer practised. Sati was presented by its proponents as an act of ultimate piety and purity. Critics of the custom have commented that the alternatives for a widow were bleak: to be effectively shunned by society – shaving her head, eating only rice and refusing social contact – and potentially mistreated by her husband's surviving family, who would inherit his property on her death.

**Post-colonial** is sometimes used to describe the period of time after colonial rule. Post-colonial studies is a branch of the social sciences that addresses the human impact of colonial rule from the perspective of native people who lived under imperialism.

A   This depiction of the practice of sati (or suttee), in which the wife of a deceased man immolates herself on her husband's funeral pyre, was painted by an Indian artist during the 19th century.

A

In the West, feminist movements have challenged dominant assertions that gender is biologically determined, and evidence to support them strengthened throughout the 20th century.

# Work on gender socialization shows that gendered behaviour is learnt, not innate.

The attitudes of those close to us as we grow up can affect how we live. Studies on gender socialization have shown that we praise particular behaviours in girls and boys, encourage specifically gendered toys and activities, and expect differentiated bodily presentations. Research also emphasizes that wider social structures are key to constructing gender difference. The weight of history, religion and what is presented as 'natural' pushes us, as a society and as individuals, towards maintaining traditional gender roles. Research into gender and education reveals systemic expectations that girls or boys will perform better or worse in particular subjects, leading them to choose – or even be encouraged to choose – different subjects at school based on their gender.

B

A This photograph is titled 'Seowoo and Her Pink Things'. It is part of the *Pink and Blue Project* (2005–ongoing) by South Korean photographer JeongMee Yoon. The series examines the relationship between gender and children's consumption in the USA and South Korea.

B 'Kihun and His Blue Things' is from the same series. 'I wanted to show the extent to which children and their parents, knowingly or unknowingly, are influenced by advertising and popular culture,' Yoon says. 'Blue has become a symbol of strength and masculinity, while pink symbolizes sweetness and femininity.'

# Studies of gender and the media have addressed how gender difference is coded in cultural representations: media products for and about boys tend to emphasize activity and bravery, whereas those for girls tend to emphasize kindness and beauty.

**Gender socialization** is a term developed within sociology and gender studies to describe the processes of learning the norms and values traditionally associated with one's gender.

In her essay 'Throwing Like a Girl: A Phenomenology of Feminine Body Comportment Motility and Spatiality' (1980), feminist philosopher Iris Marion Young (1949–2006) suggests that girls internalize the view that their bodies are weak. They may not see themselves as capable of physical tasks, which leads them not to practise at physical activities. Without practice at, for example, throwing, strength and physical confidence do not grow. Girls, Young argues, are not encouraged to use their bodies as freely as boys and this impacts throughout their life. According to Young, girls are 'physically inhibited, confined, positioned and objectified'.

An important extension of the gender socialization theories of the 1980s is Judith Butler's assertion that sex, as well as gender, is socially and culturally constructed. It is not bodily differences that matter, she says, but the way in which these come to be seen in society.

For Butler, both gender and sex are constructed through discourse. From this perspective, gender does not exist outside of discourse. Butler argues that no one is born one gender. Rather, she suggests that we learn to 'do' gender: 'We act and walk and speak and talk in ways that consolidate an impression of being a man or being a woman.'

A

A   'The Son' front page of the British newspaper *The Sun* was designed by Grey agency, London, to mark the birth of Prince George, son of the Duke and Duchess of Cambridge, in July 2013. It highlights the importance of the gender of a newborn baby in many societies, particularly when property or titles are passed down the male line.

B   After the birth of a baby in Italy, it is traditional to hang a pink rosette ribbon on the door of a household in which a girl has been born and a blue ribbon on one where a boy has been born, to announce the baby's gender.

B

Butler developed the concept of 'performativity' to consider how the rules of gender are compulsively and repetitively acted out in ways that suggest they are natural. She uses the example of the birth of a baby. When the doctor or nurse proclaims a baby is a girl or boy, they are not, says Butler, commenting on something that already exists. There is, according to Butler, no naturally gendered body. Rather, this 'speech act' – what Butler calls a 'performative utterance' – brings the gender of the child into being. The statement 'It's a girl', or 'It's a boy', inscribes gender onto the child's body. For Butler, it is societal norms and values around gender that are central to how gender is performed.

# The ways society expects us to perform our gender do not always follow a smooth linear route of progression, with improved equality and rights for both genders over time.

For example, in Iran, the rights of girls and women decreased and their prescribed social roles altered as a new government and state of power came into being in the 1980s. At the beginning of the 20th century, Iranian women were educated and fully immersed in working life. Many were involved in politics and public offices. They were often employed as journalists and writers and, as early as 1907, set up a journal focusing on women's issues. This was more than ten years before British women could vote.

However, the Iranian Revolution in 1979 saw the Islamic Republic of Iran come to power. Led by Ayatollah Khomeini, the new power-base revoked a wide range of women's rights that previously had been won by feminist movements and made sweeping changes to gender roles. Women were no longer able to take up jobs in public office, the age restriction for marriage of girls was lowered to nine years, married girls were not allowed to attend school, sex segregation was enforced in public spaces, and women were forced to follow the Islamic dress code.

# It was not until the installation of a new government nearly 20 years later, in 1997, that Iranian women began to regain their rights.

Many women became involved again in politics and feminist campaigns, and in 2003 the Nobel Peace Prize was awarded to Shirin Ebadi, a women's rights activist. In 2012, however, another new parliament again reduced the rights of women. Furthermore, Islamic laws are enforced regardless of the government in power and can act to restrict women's rights in marriage and reproduction, curtail their personal freedom and dictate dress code (depending on how they are interpreted – see Chapter 4 for more detail regarding the hijab, for example). Today, Iranian women continue to lack many fundamental rights.

A

A   A woman in a chador window shops with a couple in Western clothes in the city of Tehran in Iran, 1961. Today, women in Iran are required to cover their heads, but the chador itself is not mandatory.

B   This still is from *Fervor* (2000) by Shirin Neshat. The video art examines the themes of love and gender in Iran since the Islamic Revolution in 1979, which enforced the separation of men and women in public spaces.

**Ayatollah Khomeini** (1902–89) was an Iranian politician, Shia Muslim religious leader and vocal critic of the shah and Western influence in Iran. After the collapse of the shah's government in 1979, he declared Iran to be an Islamic republic.

**Shirin Ebadi** (b. 1947) is a lawyer, university professor and activist who has campaigned widely for human rights in Iran and worldwide. Before the Iranian Revolution, she was one of the first women to be appointed chief justice in Iran. She established the One Million Signatures campaign.

B

# Nevertheless, the women's rights movement in Iran is strong.

In 2006 it launched the campaign 'One Million Signatures for the Repeal of Discriminatory Laws' and it continues to advocate for women's rights across society.

The example of Iran shows that understandings of gender are deeply tied up with changing political and religious systems, which structure everyday gendered experiences.

The views of the political and religious leaders are in marked contrast to the beliefs of those involved in the women's rights movement. There are clearly conflicting concepts of gender, and its meanings fluctuate over time. Such conflicts demonstrate that gender is not only subject to variation across historical periods or cultures, but also fluid within a country at a particular time.

# Understandings of maleness, and expectations of what it means to be a man, are equally subject to historical and cultural variation.

In Western countries, physical attachment between men is read as a sign of same-sex attraction, and often discriminated against, but in many Arab countries it is common for heterosexual men to hold hands in public. Despite the Western construction of masculinity as the gender of strength, power and the ability to protect and provide, as we look around the globe, male roles, like female roles, can be seen to be fluid and changeable rather than fixed.

A   This photograph shows a traditional Cong Chien performance by the E De people in the Central Highlands area of Vietnam.

B   Two shepherds are pictured in 2009 near the Kokcha River in Takhar Province, Afghanistan, where it is customary for men to hold hands.

C   US President George W. Bush follows Saudi custom and holds hands with Crown Prince Abdullah in 2005, amid calls for peace in the Middle East.

A

The **E De** people are an ethnic group living in southern Vietnam, also known as the Rade or Ede. They are matrilineal, with family units living together in a longhouse owned by the most senior women in the family.

B

C

On Orango island in Guinea-Bissau, for example, men are not allowed to propose marriage, and when a woman proposes the man cannot decline. In the E De culture in southern Vietnam, men do not inherit property. There, on marriage, a man takes his wife's surname and moves into her home. In Japan, men can customarily expect to be bought gifts such as chocolates and flowers by women, and not the other way around.

Despite clear cultural and historical differences in male and female gender roles, traditional expectations for both men and women continue to structure inequalities today.

Since the Industrial Revolution, the number of women in the mainstream workforce, either supporting themselves or contributing to their family income, has increased hugely. Middle- and upper-class women, as well as working-class women, are now a routine part of the public sphere in many parts of the world, and attitudes to women in the workplace and men in the home have become more positive in many countries (see Chapter 4).

A

However, gender disparity in domestic work and childcare still remains. A survey by the British Office for National Statistics in 2016 found that in relationships in which both the woman and the man work, on average women were doing almost 40% more unpaid work in the home than men, including chores such as cleaning, shopping and cooking.

UNICEF points to the ways in which gender socialization and gendered stereotypes in many parts of the world place greater importance on the birth of boy children than that of girls, positioning boys as more valuable. According to UNICEF, this leads to girls facing discrimination in social and health care, as well as in education.

Traditional gender roles seem to have emerged to fulfil the needs of early agrarian societies. However, the extent to which these roles fluctuate depending on economic, social and political realities implies that they are based on more than fixed attributes determined by biology – that gender, in fact, is socially constructed.

# Gendered norms, values, roles and expectations are assigned by a particular society or culture and presented as ideal characteristics.

By extension, they are perpetuated by the structures and learnt values of that society – and, consciously or unconsciously, by the individuals who populate it. Since these roles and expectations are themselves what we understand as gender, and they do not remain consistent between different cultures and eras, we can argue that gender itself does not remain consistent.

Its mutability and its origin as a social construct are demonstrated partly by inconsistencies in gender role and presentation within groups of those who identify as male or female. However, the existence of transgender and non-binary gender identities also shows that traditional roles and expectations fail to account for the meanings and experiences of gender. Non-binary identities, and ideas about gender presentation as fluid rather than a compulsory social function, will be discussed in Chapter 3.

A   This Chinese family planning propaganda poster from 1986 was aimed at implementing the national one child policy.

B   A mother cries after dropping off her child at a baby hatch in Guangzhou, Guangdong province of China in 2014. Baby hatches were introduced in an attempt to discourage parents from abandoning infants on the streets. Baby daughters were at greater risk of abandonment or infanticide; they were seen as more of a burden to parents, and the one child policy prevented families from later producing a son. The policy was dropped in late 2015.

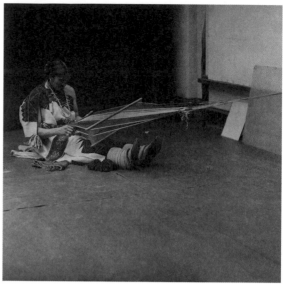

A

This chapter examines individuals and groups whose gender identities and/or expressions fall outside or cross over traditional gender roles, demonstrating that the traditional social construct of gender as a 'choice' between male or female is often incompatible with the experiences, identities and decisions of people in everyday society.

Gender systems in the West have largely followed a binary model, in which male and female are understood to be the only gender categories, with women and men seen as fundamentally different. A consideration of gender systems across the globe shows that this has not been the case elsewhere.

Historically, there have been numerous communities of people whose gender practices differ from a model of gender as only male or female. Gender diversity in India, for example, has a vivid tradition in mythology and a long history in society. Writer

**Gender systems** assign different activities, roles and positions to men and women within a particular society.

**Hijra** is a South Asian term describing a person assigned male sex at birth but who identifies and lives as female. Historically, many hijra communities have existed in South Asia and they continue to be part of contemporary society.

**Third gender** is a legal or social gender category that is neither male nor female. It exists in societies that historically have had a traditional gender role of this kind, and in societies that have recently recognized the rights of some of their members to identify as neither male nor female.

# Jacob Ogles notes in his article '19 LGBT Hindu Gods' (2016): 'For centuries, Hindu literature, mythology and religious texts have featured deities that defied the gender binary.' The hijra community, particularly, has long been part of Indian culture.

The recorded history of the hijra includes depictions in the *Kama Sutra*, which dates back to around the 2nd century AD (scholarly opinion varies widely), as well as in the *Ramayana* (*c.* 300 BC) and the *Mahabharata* (*c.* AD 400). A 2010 study by Serena Nanda suggests that most members of hijra communities are assigned male at birth, although some are intersex individuals. She found that hijra people live in close-knit communities, forming what she terms an 'institutionalized third gender role'. Historically, hijra people were thought to be asexual and were renowned for their sacred qualities, but in contemporary Indian society many earn money through sex work and from performing certain religious blessings. In 2014 they were recognized legally as a third gender in India – although not all hijra welcomed this classification.

B

A   We-Wa was a two-spirit member of the Zuni community in North America during the 19th century. Gender diverse and intersex people have traditionally been held in high regard by Native Americans and are believed to have greater spiritual gifts.

B   This group of hijra people is from South Asia, where hijra is a term used of trans and intersex people. Although traditionally well-respected members of society, many of today's hijra suffer from discrimination and poverty.

A

A **travesti**, in some South American cultures, is a person who was assigned male at birth but identifies as female. Travesti often use implants or silicone injections to appear more feminine, but may not identify fully as women or as men, rather claiming a separate gender identity with its own rules.

**Muxe** is a gender identity among the Zapotec, a minority indigenous Mexican culture. Muxe people are assigned male at birth, but assume some attributes seen as female, such as dressing in feminine clothes, wearing make-up or undertaking traditionally feminine tasks such as embroidery. They are seen as a third gender, combining male bodies with both masculine and feminine characteristics.

**Mahu**, literally meaning 'in the middle', is a third-gender identity in Hawaiian and Tahitian cultures. Mahu individuals have traditionally been respected for their ability to acknowledge both their masculine and feminine aspects, and have had a specific and valued role within society.

# Other cultures, too, have recognized the existence of more than two genders.

The travesti have a long history in many parts of Latin America. Historically, travesti have been understood as people who are both men and women, but, today, like the hijra in India, they are often considered as a third gender. In the Zapotec culture in Mexico, the muxe have been recognized traditionally as a third gender in a system predating Spanish colonization, although today the word is sometimes used as a synonym for transsexual. The mahu have traditional status in some Polynesian cultures, while in Samoan society the fa'afafine have a specific cultural role; traditionally, if a family unit did not contain enough girls to help with household work, a male child was raised as fa'afafine, displaying both masculine and feminine traits. The term 'kathoey' refers to gender-diverse people in Thailand and Laos, and gender diversity has also been documented in China, Iran, Indonesia, Japan, Nepal, South Korea and Vietnam. In Indonesia, which has the world's largest population of Muslims, waria people, who were assigned male at birth, live openly as women.

**Fa'afafine** is a recognized gender identity in Samoa for people assigned male at birth who either choose or are chosen by their family to be raised as a girl, especially if the family has a large number of sons and no daughters. Fa'afafine take on feminine attributes and have a specific social role within the family, performing tasks traditionally designated to women. Some, but not all, fa'afafine identify as female.

The **waria** are a community of third-gender people in Indonesia who are assigned male at birth but believe they are born with the souls of women. The waria community also includes people who might be considered effeminate gay men in the West. Many waria do not wish to have gender affirmation surgery for religious reasons.

The term '**two spirit**' describes indigenous North Americans in the many mixed gender roles and groups found traditionally among numerous Native American and Canadian First Nations indigenous tribes. Two spirit has replaced the older term 'berdache', which was rejected due to its initial use by colonialists.

## In discussions of gender diversity, it is important to contextualize gender within localized understandings and practices.

For example, a wide range of gender-diverse communities, such as the Zuñi La'mana, winkte, alyhaa and hwamee, has traditionally existed within various Native American tribes. Members of these communities were initially referred to as 'berdache' by early French explorers ('berdache' was a French term for the younger partner in a male homosexual relationship), and then more widely by colonizers. Today, they generally prefer to be recognized in English as **two-spirit** people, a favoured umbrella term given the colonial and pejorative connotations of berdache. Historically, two-spirit people were usually valued by their tribes, who saw them as being blessed with both a masculine and a feminine spirit, although during the 20th century Euro-American and Christian influences disrupted this tradition.

A   A trans woman marries her boyfriend in 2002 in Juchitán, Mexico, a matriarchal fishing village where gender diversity is accepted.

B   A member of the waria community applies make-up during the Syawalan tradition in Yogyakarta, Indonesia, in 2015.

B

A

# Until the late 20th century, anthropological studies often interpreted gender-diverse practices as personifications of same-sex desire.

Some studies focusing on Native American gender-diverse communities read these cultural traditions as representing homosexual lifestyles, particularly because two-spirit people who were biologically male but took on feminine characteristics often married masculine men, and vice versa. Some gay and lesbian members of Native American tribes choose to describe themselves as two-spirit people, aligning themselves with a cultural tradition of respect for alternative sexual or gendered lifestyles. Other anthropologists who instead represent them as transsexual cultures have questioned the positioning of the two-spirit people as gay forefathers.

B

Yet 'transsexual' is a relatively recent Western concept. As more contemporary accounts have suggested, it is probable that two-spirit people represented neither same-sex nor transgender practices, but, instead, demonstrated the existence of an alternative gender or sexual grouping within an indigenous culture of which there is no Western equivalent.

The confusion of gender-diverse practices with homosexuality is a common one, particularly in Western cultures.

A    A group of hijras dance together as they prepare
     backstage for a talent show as part of 'Hijra Pride
     2014', a third sex parade launched to campaign the
     Bangladesh government to recognize hijra identities.
B    The Bandhu Social Welfare Society organized 'Hijra
     Pride 2014'. Here, two hijras prepare for the parade.

A

Part of this confusion stems from the fact that gender and sexuality are seen as closely linked by many societies. A transgender person who chooses to transition from male to female, but who remains attracted to women throughout her transition, has, in the eyes of society, transitioned not only from male to female but also from straight to gay – despite the fact that her sexual orientation has not actually changed.

Another factor may have been the early stages of the development of sexology in Europe and the USA in the 20th century, which, in studying human sexuality, also brought about new ways of understanding gender-diverse people.

In pre-industrial Europe the regulation of sexual behaviour, like that of moral behaviour, was considered to be a religious or spiritual issue and fell under the remit of the Church. Sexology marked a move away from understanding sexuality through religious and moral frameworks, as it became the subject of scientific enquiry. Through the 19th century, doctors and scientists became the dominant instructors in communities and courts about sexual normality and sexual deviance. In his book *The History of Sexuality* (1976), philosopher Michel Foucault (1926–84) argues that during this time there was a redefinition of sexuality according to type and identity rather than acts and behaviour.

# Rather than being something we did, sexuality became a key facet of who we are.

Such ways of thinking about sexuality reflected a binary biological model. Sexuality became classified through a duality of 'normal' and 'deviant'; reproductive heterosexual sex in marriage was the norm, and other sexualities were constructed as deviant opposites. An array of sexual practices was pathologized. Cross-dressing and cross-living gender practices were initially understood within the same framework as homosexuality. Homosexuality, and, by turn, gender diversity were seen to be an inferior imitation of heterosexuality, emerging as a result of biological deficiency. Homosexuality and anal intercourse had historically often been criminalized or constructed as unnatural, but with sexology came medicalization, pathologization and a medical rationale for presenting both homosexuality and gender diversity as deviant.

A

B

# The idea of the invert was significant in sexological thinking.

Sexual inversion was believed to signify an inborn reversal of gender traits: male inverts were inclined to traditionally female pursuits and dress, and vice versa. This understanding is evident in the work of prominent sexologist Henry Havelock Ellis (1859–1939), published in seven volumes titled *Studies in the Psychology of Sex* (1897–1928). Inversion, he said, represented 'sexual instinct turned by inborn constitutional abnormality toward persons of the same sex'. In a similar vein, sexologist Richard von Krafft-Ebing (1840–1902) described homosexuality in 1898 as resulting from female sexual inversion, 'the masculine soul, heaving in the female bosom'. Within early sexology, gender and sexuality were seen to be inherently connected: the male homosexual was artistic and effeminate; the lesbian, artistic and mannish.

The concept of sexual inversion soon gained currency in wider society and was evident in cultural representations, as exemplified in *The Well of Loneliness* (1928) by Radclyffe Hall (1880–1943).

A   Irish novelist, poet and playwright Oscar Wilde was convicted in London in 1895 of sodomy and imprisoned after letters to his male lover were made public. He served ten years' hard labour in Reading prison.
B   *Self-portrait* (1928) by Claude Cahun. Cahun's work portrayed a variety of gender diverse personas.

C   Radclyffe Hall is seen here with Una Vincenzo, Lady Troubridge in 1927. Hall and Troubridge lived together as a couple in London and East Sussex. Hall was best known for her semi-autobiographical novel *The Well of Loneliness*. It depicted sexual inversion, a 19th-century conflation of trans and homosexual identities.

The novel tells the story of 'invert' Stephen Gordon: assigned female at birth, she longs to be a boy and becomes a more androgynous or gender-neutral character as she grows older, also developing a romantic relationship with a woman, Mary. As described in the novel, Stephen 'hated her body with its muscular shoulders, its small compact breasts, and its slender flanks of an athlete. All her life she must drag this body of hers like a monstrous fetter imposed on her spirit.' The preface was written by Havelock Ellis: 'It is the first English novel which presents, in a completely faithful and uncompromising form, one particular aspect of sexual life as it exists among us today.'

# In the novel, we see the influence of sexology in two key aspects: first, in the idea of the lesbian as an invert; second, in the way in which gender and sexuality were coupled.

During this time, sexological works and cultural forms concerning non-heterosexual or gender-diverse practices were considered obscene and prosecuted under the Obscene Publications Act of 1857. On publication, *The Well of Loneliness* was banned in Britain under the Act, the judge at the trial stating: 'I have no hesitation whatsoever in saying that it is an obscene libel, that it would tend to corrupt those into whose hands it should fall, and that the publication of this book is an offence against public decency...'

**Invert** is a term developed in the early study of sexology to refer to homosexual men or lesbian women. In presenting homosexuality as an inner reversal of a person's exterior gender traits, the word conflates gender with sexuality.

c

Gender-diverse practices were not subject to legal regulation at this time, but gender diversity became incorporated into what Foucault conceptualized as the medicalization of the sexually 'peculiar'.

Although cross-dressing practices and cross-gender expressions have a long history, medical studies did not coin the term 'transvestism' until 1910, and later 'transsexuality' in 1950.

*Transvestites* (1910), a seminal study by sexologist Magnus Hirschfeld (1868–1935), classified the practice of cross-dressing.

A

A The prominent sexologist Magnus
Hirschfeld is pictured with his partner
at a party at the Institute of Sexology.
Hirschfeld is second from the right,
with moustache and glasses; his
partner, museum curator Karl Giese,
holds his hand.
B During the 1930s and 1940s,
trans women and male cross-
dressers were frequently arrested
for homosexuality. This image is by
New York photographer Weegee.

B

In it, he defined transvestism as 'the impulse
to assume the external garb of a sex which
is not apparently that of the subject as indicated
by the sexual organs'. Havelock Ellis also argued
against the prevalent correlation of same-sex
desire and cross-dressing.

# Cross-dressing and cross-gender living practices became the focus of medical intervention, which was both diagnostic and curative.

As discussed in previous chapters, gender-
diverse or intersex individuals can have a unique
religious role to play in Hindu culture and some
Native American tribal cultures, among others.

Ancient Greek mythology, too, includes numerous references to androgyny, cross-gender practices and intersex; for example, portrayals of the god Aphroditus – an incarnation of the more commonly portrayed female Aphrodite – show him/her as having both breasts and a penis. Various contemporary sources claim that during sacrifices to Aphroditus, men and women would exchange clothing and gender roles.

Outside the world of religion, the history of cross-dressing in the theatre stretches back at least as far as ancient Greece, where male actors played the parts of both women and men. Japanese kabuki theatre and Yuan dynasty Chinese opera both featured cross-dressing. The same was also true in Renaissance England; several of Shakespeare's plays, including *The Merchant of Venice*, *As You Like It* and *Twelfth Night*, take advantage of this by featuring female characters (who would have been played by male actors) dressing as men – a double deception. A century after Shakespeare, in the 1700s, it was common for upper-class men to wear elaborately decorated clothing, wigs, make-up and jewelry. Such embellishments did not suggest homosexuality, as later became the case, but wealth and prestige.

A

**Androgyny** is a combination of characteristics considered masculine and characteristics considered feminine. It is most often used to describe a person or thing with no gender, mixed gender or ambiguous gender.

A   In this Japanese portrait of two kabuki actors in the 1890s – one playing a woman, the other a samurai – both figures wear make-up and are heavily adorned. Traditionally, both male and female parts are played by men in kabuki theatre.

B   This work by 19th-century English painter and book illustrator Richard Frederick Pickersgill depicts Duke Orsino and his lover Viola (disguised as a boy), from Shakespeare's comedy *Twelfth Night*. In Renaissance England, it was common for male actors to play female roles; Viola's cross-dressing allowed for an additional layer of complication.

B

There are also historical instances of women who cross-dressed and lived as men in order to access male occupations or pastimes that were unavailable to women.

A well-known (but possibly fictional) example is that of Hua Mulan in northern China, said to have dressed as a man in order to help her elderly father avoid the draft. In Britain, Hannah Snell (1723–92) enlisted in the Royal Marines under the name of James Gray and fought as a soldier between 1747 and 1750. Snell left the army after being wounded and received a military pension. On the death of jazz musician Billy Tipton (1914–89) in the USA, it became apparent he had the body of someone assigned female at birth. Tipton, it is believed, had decided early in his adult life that he would have greater opportunities and success as a man than as a woman.

A MORNING FROLIC, or the TRANSMUTATION of SEXES.
From the Original Picture by John Collet, in the possession of Carington Bowles.

A    Titled *A Morning Frolic, or the Transmutation of the Sexes* (c. 1780), this work by an unknown artist (after John Collett) shows a soldier and a woman *en déshabille* (in a state of undress), after swapping items of clothing.

B    These two portraits of Lili Elbe in c. 1928 are attributed to her wife, the Danish artist Gerda Wegener. In 1930 Elbe had what is recognized as the first instance of gender reassignment surgery at the Institute of Sexology in Berlin. The surgery was supervised by prominent sexologist Magnus Hirschfeld. After the surgery, Elbe's marriage was annulled because the law failed to recognize the marriage of two women.

There have been varying degrees of space within society for such practices. Sexual historians such as Ian McCormick have documented how, during the 18th and 19th centuries, clubs known as molly houses provided a space for men to dress as women. During the 1920s, several influential writers, artists and philosophers – including Virginia Woolf (1882–1941), Radclyffe Hall and Gluck (1895–1978) – presented androgynously, wearing the clothes of middle-class men of the time: suit, shirt, waistcoat and tie, and brogue shoes.

From the 1930s, advancements in medical technology in Western Europe made available what were then termed 'sex change' operations, bringing the possibility of not only cross-living and cross-dressing, but also of physically altering the body.

Danish painter Lili Elbe (1882–1931) was one of the first publicly known trans women to undergo gender affirmation surgery (as it is now known), initially under the supervision of Magnus Hirschfeld in Germany.

# Body modification was part of broader changes in understandings of gendered embodiment and identity.

As access to surgical procedures became more readily accessible in the 1960s, the term 'transsexual' was popularized to describe individuals undergoing surgery. This period also witnessed the growth of US research into transgender practices. *The Transsexual Phenomenon* (1966) by Harry Benjamin (1885–1986), *Sex and Gender* (1968) by Robert Stoller (1924–91) and *Transsexualism and Sex Reassignment* (1969) by Richard Green (b. 1936) and John Money (1921–2006) are the most notable examples.

# Apparent in each of these texts was the notion that transsexual people were born in the 'wrong body'.

Surgery was positioned as the appropriate treatment, bringing the body in alignment with gender identity. What did not change was the understanding of gender diversity as pathological.

In *Transmen and FTMs* (1999), trans male writer Jason Cromwell describes his initial search for information about transition: 'The research was to point out my error regarding the possibility of getting hormones and having surgery unless I was willing to admit to a diseased mind (psychosis, neurosis, schizophrenia and delusions, as well as perversion, bouts of depression and paranoia) and submit to surgical mutilation.'

A

A   Students march on Hirschfeld's Institute of Sexology in Berlin. In 1933 the German Student Union declared action against the un-German spirit. The students burnt scientific texts and literature, which they believed degraded German purity. This foreshadowed the move towards Nazism.
B   In 1950 George Jorgensen left New York for a series of gender reassignment surgeries in Denmark. These images exemplify the media's fixation with 'before' and 'after' narratives of transition, which still remains today.

BEFORE    AFTER    TODAY

B

Despite significant changes in under-standings of sexuality and gender since the early 20th century, the model that was constructed through sexology has been hard to shift.

Understandings of gender and sexuality continue to be intertwined and sexuality is still connected to gender in many contemporary understandings.

For example, sociobiologists such as Simon LeVay (b. 1943) propose the 'gay gene' theory, which suggests that same-sex orientation in men results from differences in the size of certain cells in the brain. Dean Hamer (b. 1951) also proposes a biological model of sexual behaviour in his genetic theory, which claims that gay men have fewer X chromosomes than heterosexual men. This links male homosexuality with facets of male biological sex, implying that gay men are genetically more 'feminine' than straight men.

The idea that gay men are 'born this way' finds favour in some sections of the LGBTQI community, who use the theory to argue against discrimination.

Yet there are many opponents of a biological model of sexuality, just as there are opponents of a biological model of gender.

In the 1940s and 1950s, US sexologist Alfred Kinsey (1894–1956) published the 'Kinsey Reports', which proposed that sexuality lay on a continuum. While some people were firmly at one end (heterosexual) or the other (gay/lesbian), many people, he said, were at different points on the continuum (bisexual). People, he argues in *Sexual Behaviour in the Human Male* (1948), 'do not represent two discrete populations, heterosexual and homosexual. The world is not to be divided into sheep and goats. It is a fundamental of taxonomy that nature rarely deals with discrete categories.'

Research from the social sciences also suggests that sexuality is fluid and that people can, and do, choose their sexuality.

A   Sexologist Alfred Kinsey's study *Sexual Behaviour in the Human Female* was published in 1948, along with *Sexual Behaviour in the Human Male*. Together, the works became widely known as the 'Kinsey Reports'.

B   *Oh! Dr. Kinsey!* (1953) by Lawrence Lariar was a book of photographs depicting women's comic reactions to a series of questions supposed to resemble those asked by Alfred Kinsey and his researchers.

The Kinsey Reports drew attention to the common occurrence of sex outside of marriage, same-sex practices and infidelity. They both shocked and fascinated US society during the 1950s.

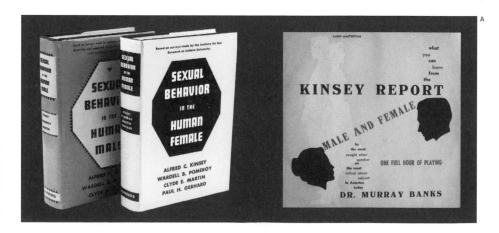

Sociologists Linda Garnets and Anne Peplau carried out research, presented in 2006, into women's sexuality and found that, rather than being fixed, women's sexual orientation is flexible. It is, they argue, shaped by life experiences and social and cultural factors such as 'women's education, social status and power, economic opportunities and attitudes about women's roles'. From this viewpoint, sexual identity, desire and practices can change across a person's lifetime, as can gender identity and experience.

# Both gender and sexuality could be thought of as existing along a spectrum, or perhaps two separate but intimately related spectra.

However, this analogy leaves out the experiences of people who are asexual or agender, both terms that have gained currency in recent years.

LGBTQI is an acronym for lesbian, gay, bisexual, transgender, queer (or questioning), intersex. Other letters or symbols can be added in order to make the acronym more inclusive, such as 'A' for asexual or agender, or '*' to acknowledge a range of possible identities and sexual orientations.

An asexual person experiences little or no sexual desire or attraction. Asexuality is a sexual orientation, like heterosexuality or homosexuality. Asexual people may or may not feel romantic attraction, which is not the same as sexual attraction.

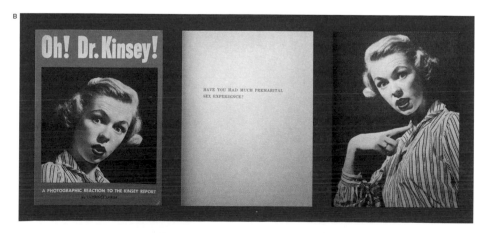

B

A

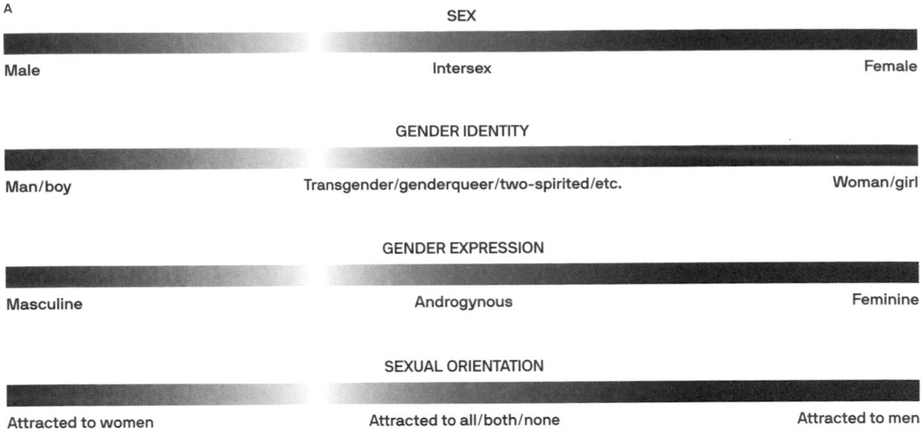

SEX

Male                              Intersex                            Female

GENDER IDENTITY

Man/boy        Transgender/genderqueer/two-spirited/etc.        Woman/girl

GENDER EXPRESSION

Masculine                       Androgynous                       Feminine

SEXUAL ORIENTATION

Attracted to women        Attracted to all/both/none        Attracted to men

While asexual orientation is probably not new, the Internet has enabled the development of asexual communities, the largest of which is the Asexual Visibility and Education Network, founded in 2001, with the goals of 'creating public acceptance and discussion of asexuality and facilitating the growth of an asexual community'. As such, there is a push by some in the asexual community for the letter 'A' to be added to the acronym LGBTQI to make asexuality visible as a sexual identity.

# Correspondingly, the term 'agender' is used by people to signify that they do not feel they have a gender identity.

A   Alfred Kinsey argued that his study showed that rather than representing a binary of homosexuality versus heterosexuality, human sexuality operated on a spectrum. These spectrums show different aspects of gender functioning in a similar way. Such linear visualisations still refer to a gender binary, implying that non-binary genders fall between the two poles of male or female.

B   This non-linear figure depicts gender identity as a series of possibilities that can overlap or interact with each other, rather than as a binary model of male and female.

C   This figure shows some possible relationships between sex and sexuality, including male, female and intersex variations. However, it does not refer to asexuality.

B

Agender

Masculine agender

Feminine agender

1

Male

2

Uncertain and/or all

3

Female

Masculine genderfluid

4

Feminine genderfluid

Genderfluid

1 Genderfluid agender
2 Uncertain and/or agender/genderfluid masculine/genderqueer
3 Uncertain and/or agender/genderfluid/feminine/genderqueer
4 Genderfluid agender

C

PERSON'S SEX IS NOT SPECIFIED

Androphilic

Gynephilic

Androphilic (homosexual) male

Ambiphilic

Gynephilic (homosexual) female

Male

Ambiphilic (bisexual) male

Ambiphilic (bisexual) female

Female

Ambiphilic (bisexual) intersex

Gynephilic (heterosexual) male

Androphilic (heterosexual) female

1

2

Intersex

PERSON'S SEXUALITY IS NOT SPECIFIED

1 Gynephilic intersex
2 Androphilic intersex

When we include agender and asexual identities, which are by their definition 'off the spectrum', as well as identities such as genderfluid and genderflux, it can make more sense to think of both gender identity and sexual orientation as the combination of a complex constellation of traits that can vary widely from person to person. Individual traits may be 'more feminine', 'more masculine' or neither; or 'more heterosexual', 'more homosexual' or neither. A person might have many gender-related traits that are 'more masculine' but some that are 'more feminine' (or vice versa), an even balance or many 'gender-neutral' traits – and likewise with traits associated with sexuality. Collected together, these traits form a person's gender identity and sexual orientation. As understanding of this issue increases, the wide variety of possible combinations could help explain the recent proliferation of terms used to describe gender identity and sexual orientation.

As awareness of the complexity of gender increases, the notion of gender as fluid has become more prevalent and has entered British and US celebrity culture. Actress and singer Miley Cyrus (b. 1992) discussed gender identity as fluid and asserts: '[Today] you can just be whatever you want to be.' In an interview with *Out* magazine, Cyrus explains further: 'I don't relate to what people would say defines a girl or a boy, and I think that's what I had to understand: being a girl isn't what I hate, it's the box that I get put into.'

A

Actress Tilda Swinton (b. 1960) also resists definition as either female or male, saying in a recent interview: 'I don't know if I could ever really say that I was a girl – I was kind of a boy for a long time. I don't know, who knows? It changes.' Australian actress and model Ruby Rose (b. 1986) similarly states: 'I am very genderfluid and feel more like I wake up every day sort of gender neutral.'

JD Samson (b. 1978), band member of Le Tigre and MEN, talks of being 'post-gender' and discusses the female/male gender binary as outdated. It is not only younger people who are articulating their gender as fluid: comedian Eddie Izzard (b. 1962), for example, talks of being 'a complete boy plus half girl', artist Grayson Perry (b. 1960) often appears as his alter ego Claire, and musician Pete Townshend (b. 1945) has said: 'I know how it feels to be a woman because I am a woman. And I won't be classified as just a man.' Outside of Britain, Australia and the USA, prominent figures are also articulating non-binary gender identifications, including Brazilian model Lea T (b. 1981) and Canadian author Rae Spoon (b. 1982).

## Despite the increasing recognition of gender diversity, it can still be a controversial topic.

# In particular, gender discomfort among children is an issue that has caused medical concern, gained cultural visibility and provoked discussion.

Although not all children conform or internalize the limitations of gender stereotypes, those who do not act in accordance with gendered norms may be subjected to isolation from peers or be reprimanded by teachers or parents. This can lead to young people having low self-esteem and committing acts of self-harm and even suicide. A report by campaigning charity Stonewall, for example, found that eight out of ten young LGBTQ people have self-harmed and have attempted suicide as a result of bullying. They are also more likely to be affected by homelessness.

B

A   British musician David Bowie is seen here in 1971 with his wife Angie and three-week-old son Zowie. He is wearing an Oxford Bags dress, Turkish cotton shirt and a felt hat. The widely published photographs, by Ron Burton, show both parents challenging gender boundaries.

B   Seen here at The Guardian Hay Festival in 2004, Claire is the female alter ego of Turner Prize-winning artist Grayson Perry. He has been cross-dressing since childhood and has developed increasingly flamboyant expressions for Claire. 'I think of my dressing up as the heraldry of my subconscious,' he says.

The Gender Identity Development Service (GIDS) in London specializes in counselling children who are concerned about their gender. In 1982, the year it opened, GIDS had two referrals. In 2015–2016, referrals were at 1,400, having doubled since the previous year. Of these, nearly 300 were for children under the age of 12. In Canada, 2016 saw a 600% increase in applications to the Family Court by young people who wanted their gender recognized as other than that ascribed at birth. Cultural visibility and changing social attitudes have meant that families, schools and children themselves have a greater knowledge of gender diversity.

In Sweden, for example, policy against discrimination on the grounds of gender diversity has led to the development of gender-neutral preschools, which adopt a non-gendered stance in all that they teach. Books with gender stereotypes are not used, all children are encouraged to take equal part in all activities, and the non-gendered pronoun 'hen' is as common as 'he' or 'she'. This approach is favoured by a number of professionals specializing in gender identity among children, including those at GIDS. A move to recognize gender diversity in children has, however, proved hugely controversial.

A

From one perspective, children are naturally gender diverse; it is only society that imposes a gender-binary system on them. From this position, the increasing numbers of children concerned about their gender being referred to support services can be read as a long-overdue sign that gender-diverse children are now being given the attention they need.

**In other words, children as a whole have not become more likely to be transgender; rather, transgender children are no longer suffering in silence.**

A   These photographs are from an ongoing series by Dutch photographer Sarah Wong titled *Inside Out: Portraits of Cross-Gender Children*. From left to right: 'Princess on White Horse', 'Girl', 'Boy with Swimming Suit' and 'Boy'. The project was created in 2003 when Wong began to follow a group of Dutch transgender children as they each sought a new identity. 'Every girl you see in these photographs was born male, and every boy was born female,' says the artist.

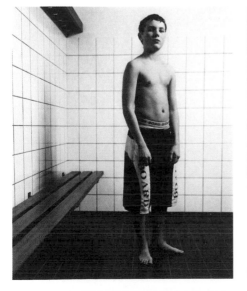

A

# From another position, there is cause for concern.

Arguing that children cannot have a developed understanding of these issues, some are fiercely opposed to the idea that children may identify as gender diverse. John Whitehall, professor of paediatrics at Western Sydney University, has suggested that diagnosis of gender dysphoria amounts to child abuse. This is, he continues, a 'massive intrusion into the minds and bodies of children'. President Trump's judicial nominee Jeff Mateer has been outspoken within these debates in the USA, notoriously saying that transgender children are part of 'Satan's plan'.

From members of indigenous third-gender communities to those across the globe who have historically cross-dressed, and from the development of cross-gender body modification technologies to proclamations of non-binary gender, this chapter has shown that gender may be experienced diversely and practised fluidly at individual and subjective levels.

What clearly emerges is that whatever we mean when we talk about gender – whether it is biological sex, a socially constructed role we perform, a personal identity or a combination of all three – it is fluid.

# Biological sex is not entirely restricted to male or female.

Socialized gender roles are not fixed or consistent either within different eras and cultures, or within one society at one time. People's gender identities are not always consistent with social norms, or unchanging throughout their lifetimes. As increasing numbers of people become aware of this, gender activism and advocacy movements are on the rise. These instances of collective and individual gendered agency will be discussed in Chapter 4.

**Gender dysphoria** is a medical term used to describe the experience of feeling that one's emotional and embodied identity is different to that which was assigned at birth.

A  The anti-trans 'Free Speech Bus' toured the USA in 2017, but met with resistance that included being tagged with pro-trans graffiti on its arrival in New York.
B  *I am Jazz* (2015) by Jessica Herthel, a book for children about being transgender, draws on the life experiences of Jazz Jennings, who transitioned as a child.

B

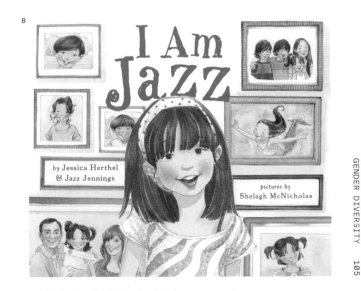

RESIST
NO!
In the Name of Human
We REFUSE To Accep
a Fascist America!
DRIVE OUT

4. Gender Activism

Club Patriotique De Femmes.
*Des Femmes bien Patriotes avoient formées en club, dans lequel netoit admise aucune autres; Elles avoient leur Présidente et des sécrataires, on s'assembloit Deux fois la semaine, La Présidente faisoit la Lecture des Séances de la convention nationnale, on approuvoit ou lon critiquoit ses Décrets, Ces Dames animées du zéle et de la Bienfaisance faisoient, entr'elles une qui étoit distribuée à des familles de bons Patriotes qui ont besoins de secours.*

A

The ***Declaration of the Rights of Woman and of the [Female] Citizen*** is a pamphlet written by Olympe de Gouges in 1791. She based it on the *Declaration of the Rights of Man and of the Citizen*, the groundbreaking declaration of civil rights adopted by the National Constituent Assembly, to expose the French Revolution's failure to recognize women's rights.

# In one sense, there has been gender activism for as long as there has been gender diversity.

Many of the instances of gender diversity mentioned in previous chapters involved individuals or communities advocating for the right to self-identify gender.

However, most current gender activism movements have their roots in the development of modern-day feminism (in Europe and the USA, from the late 18th century) and the modern trans rights movement (during the late 19th century, closely linked with early LGBTQ rights movements through sexology).

During the late 18th century, women such as Mary Wollstonecraft (see Chapter 1) and Olympe de Gouges (1748–93) began to advocate for women to be treated as equal to men. De Gouges, whose *Declaration of the Rights of Woman and of the [Female] Citizen* was published in 1791 – the year before Wollstonecraft's *A Vindication of the Rights of Women* – adjured men to examine 'sexual characteristics in the workings of nature: everywhere you will find them intermingled, everywhere cooperating harmoniously...' She was a prolific writer who saw women's rights as part of a wider range of natural human rights.

# Even in the early days of its modern incarnation, gender activism was not restricted to the actions of upper-class white women in the West.

Intersectionality was particularly important to black and post-colonial feminist writing in theorizing the intersections of gender and race. Black feminists drew attention to the ways in which black women are discriminated against in the workplace, for example, on the basis of both their race and their gender. During the early days of feminism, many activists had links to anti-slavery reform and social justice movements.

A  *Club Patriotique de Femmes (The Patriotic Women's Club)* (1791) by Jean-Baptiste Lesueur. From 1791 to 1793, French women formed groups such as the one depicted here to support the Republican regime and campaign for the same political rights as men. They are shown donating coins to support the cause.

B  These examples of anti-slavery stoneware and porcelain medallions were designed by William Hackwood of Wedgewood in 1787 for distribution by the anti-slavery movement. The inscription reads: 'Am I not a man and a brother?' The medallions became emblems of the abolitionist cause.

A   Anti-slave campaigner and women's rights activist Sojourner Truth sat for a number of portraits, printed with the slogan 'I sell the shadow to support the substance'. They affirmed her status as a 'free woman and as a woman in control of her image'.

B   This carte-de-visite shows abolitionist Harriet Tubman as a young woman during the Civil War, between 1868 and 1869.

C   Beulah Faith was an ex-sales clerk from a department store. Here, she is depicted reaming tools on a lathe machine for Consolidated Aircraft Corp., Fort Worth, Texas, in 1942.

# The historical case of Sojourner Truth brings to light the ways in which gender and race intersect to disadvantage.

She is best known for her speech 'Ain't I a Woman?', delivered at a women's rights meeting in Ohio in May 1851: 'That man over there says that women need to be helped into carriages, and lifted over ditches, and to have the best place everywhere. Nobody ever helps me into carriages, or over mud-puddles, or gives me any best place! And ain't I a woman? Look at me! Look at my arm! I have ploughed and planted, and gathered into barns, and no man could head me! And ain't I a woman? I could work as much and eat as much as a man – when I could get it – and bear the lash as well! And ain't I a woman? I have borne thirteen children, and seen most all sold off to slavery, and when I cried out with my mother's grief, none but Jesus heard me! And ain't I a woman?'

Truth's gender identity is claimed through her repeated rhetorical question, 'Ain't I a woman?'. Yet she points out that white men and women do not see her as symbolizing womanhood.

As sociologists Gail Lewis and Ann Phoenix note in 'Race, Ethnicity and Identity' (2004), 'Her short speech powerfully challenged essentialist thinking that women are necessarily weaker than men and that enslaved black women were not real women.'

As a result of the activism of women such as Truth and Harriet Tubman (*c*. 1822–1913) in the late 19th and early 20th centuries, the suffrage movement in Europe and North America challenged the exclusion of women from the electoral register.

Ideas around appropriate gender roles fluctuated during World Wars I and II, as women were needed to work in industry and manual trades to fill the gaps left by men drafted into military service. Although it was expected that women would go back to the domestic arena of the home during peace time, the experience of independence for women during the two wars began a process of change through which the fixity of gender roles – and understandings of what gender is – began to unravel. In Britain, suffrage for women over the age of 21 was won in 1928.

**Sojourner Truth** (*c*. 1797–1883) is the adopted name of a woman born in New York who escaped slavery before mandatory emancipation became law in the state in 1828. She played a significant role in the early women's rights movement.

c

This period, during which the focus was on equality of contractual and civil rights, is often referred to as first-wave feminism, and is credited with providing the impetus for the development of second-wave feminism during the late 1960s and 1970s in Britain and the USA. Activism was widespread during this period. In the USA, groups such as the National Organization for Women, the National Association for the Repeal of Abortion Laws and the Combahee River Collective focused on marital and reproductive rights, the family, equality in the work-place, sexuality and ending violence against women.

**First-wave feminism** refers to the organized feminist movements of the 19th and early 20th centuries. These usually focused on legal issues such as suffrage (the right to vote) and the right for women to own property, divorce and seek custody over children.

**Second-wave feminism** describes the period from the late 1960s to the early 1980s, during which the focus widened to include de facto inequalities, sexuality and reproductive rights.

The **Combahee River Collective** was a group of black feminists, many of whom were lesbians, who spoke out about racism in the white feminist movement. The group was active from 1974 to 1980. They created the Combahee River Collective statement, one of the first documents to call for an intersectional approach to addressing oppression.

A

Alongside second-wave feminism, organizations and publications uniting LGBTQ people and focusing on gay, lesbian and transgender rights began to reach a wider audience.

Two early pioneers in the USA were Louise Lawrence, who corresponded with a network of transgender people in Europe and the USA during the 1950s, and Virginia Prince (1912–2009), who founded the influential magazine *Transvestia* in 1960 (an earlier version, *Transvestia: The Journal of the American Society for Equality in Dress* (1952), is considered by theorists including Susan Stryker (b. 1961) to represent the beginning of the transgender rights movement in the USA). In 1969, transgender activists played a pivotal part in New York's Stonewall Riots, which brought LGBTQ rights into the wider public consciousness; an increasing number of activist organizations were established in the years after Stonewall.

**Louise Lawrence** (1912–76) was a pioneering transgender woman. She lived full-time as a woman from the early 1940s, and amassed a wide network of cross-dressers and transgender people. She also assisted researchers such as Alfred Kinsey and Harry Benjamin.

*Transvestia* is an independent magazine, aimed at heterosexual transvestites, published during the 1960s by transgender activist Virginia Prince. Its readers could submit their own stories and photographs for publication.

The **Stonewall Riots** were a series of protests and violent confrontations between police and members of the LGBT community in 1969. Sparked by a police raid on the Stonewall Inn in New York, they were a catalyst for activism.

A  Opposing views on abortion were expressed during this reproductive rights demonstration in Pittsburgh, Pennsylvania, in 1974. This followed the Supreme Court decision in Roe vs. Wade in 1973 to permit elective abortions.
B  These front covers are from *Transvestia* magazine, which, according to a 1963 edition, was 'dedicated to the needs of the sexually normal individual who has discovered the existance [sic] of his or her "other side" and seeks to express it'.

B

The #MeToo hashtag was created in 2006 by activist Tarana Burke (b. 1973), but came to prominence in 2017 as a response to numerous allegations of assault by producer Harvey Weinstein. Millions of women and men used the hashtag on social media to disclose the fact that they had experienced sexual assault or harassment.

A

The shift from understanding gender as biologically 'hard-wired' to understanding it as a flexible, mutable social construct was advanced by feminist and LGBTQ groups throughout the later decades of the 20th century. Problematizing the idea that gender roles were fixed was important to feminist movements, because it challenged the theory that inequality between men and women was in some way predetermined, and to many LGBTQ groups because it allowed for the existence of gender roles and sexual orientations outside the 'norms' of cisgender and heterosexuality.

Activism continued largely unabated throughout the second half of the 20th century, with second-wave feminism followed closely by a more diverse 'third wave' during the 1990s and 2000s. In the West, recent feminist movements (sometimes referred to as 'fourth-wave' feminism) have continued to diversify.

A  Kathleen Hanna from the US punk band Bikini Kill performs at the Macondo in Los Angeles in 1993. Bikini Kill are often cited as the pioneers of the Riot Grrrl movement and are well known for their explicitly feminist lyrics.

B  Russian conceptual artist Nadezhda Tolokonnikova performs with her band Pussy Riot in 2017 in Houston, Texas. Having begun as a guerrilla movement, the group has a varied membership and puts on impromptu politically themed public performances.

B

Drives such as the #MeToo campaign have focused on sexual violence and harassment, highlighting an imbalance in the power dynamic between men and women, particularly in the professional sphere. This ties in with issues of childcare provision and the adoption of flexible working conditions for both women and men in seeking to ensure greater levels of equality in the workplace.

Campaigns challenge the stereotypes that continue to define childcare and house-work as 'women's work', and to construct 'women's work' as inherently less valuable.

This devaluation of femininity makes it difficult for women taking on traditional gender roles to claim status equal to men, and for men to take on traditionally feminine roles or to display feminine characteristics without a perceived loss of status.

Gender stereotypes also create problems for professional women. British management and recruitment specialist Paula Parfitt speaks of an unconscious bias in recruitment processes in 2015: 'We know that female candidates tend to be judged on experience, whereas male candidates are assessed on potential, and that interviewers are more likely to question women than men on their ability to balance work and family life.'

## Gendered expectations about domestic work, as well as employ-ment in the public sphere, are changing in many countries.

Campaigns – many led by feminist movements – to ensure that childcare is seen to be the responsibility of the father as well as the mother have led to legal provision for paternity, as well as maternity, leave.

A   Swedish-based Top Toy produces gender neutral toys that challenge gender stereotyping in children's play. Its catalogue features images of children playing with toys traditionally associated with the opposite gender.
B   These gender neutral branding tags were designed by Charlie Smith Design for a line of non-gendered clothing by UK company John Lewis. In 2017 John Lewis became the first store to remove gendered clothing labels in order to challenge gender stereotyping in children's wear.

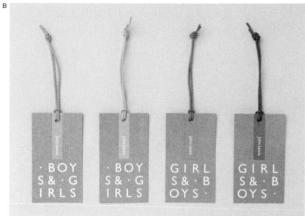

Sweden, for example, has three months' paternity provision for new fathers, compared with only two weeks' statutory leave in Britain. In Japan, both mother and father are entitled to a paid year off work. Yet policy to encourage greater gender equality does not always work due to the persistence of cultural ideas about gendered roles and stereotypes. For example, in Japan, less than 2% of men take the full year of paternity leave on offer. The USA is one of the few countries in the developed world that does not have statutory maternity or paternity leave. Government provision of childcare for mothers and fathers is therefore an issue high on the agenda of feminist movements in the USA.

Feminist campaigns have also sought to challenge gender stereotypes by providing children with un-gendered toys or clothes, and market conditions are beginning to change.

The Pinkstinks campaign addresses the stereotype that girls only desire clothes or toys that are pink. The British department store John Lewis's review of the changing market has led them to remove gender-specific labels from children's clothes. These examples are important in showing how changing understandings of gender – in this case away from rigid gender stereotyping in childhood – can impact greatly on the ways in which gender is lived.

A

Such examples also illustrate that traditional ways of understanding gender are strongly defended. John Lewis's decision to display gender-neutral children's clothes, for example, created a storm of dissenting voices on social media: 'There are only two sexes, male or female,' tweeted one angry customer, while another stated, 'My child is a boy and will be dressed as a boy...rugby tops, polo shirts, jeans...trainers etc.' As gender shifts, boundaries are drawn in defence of traditional gender roles and practices.

Understandings of gender are – as we have seen – culturally specific, and the concerns of Western feminism are not always global ones. Some have challenged the idea of global feminism, arguing that a universal approach to women's issues is problematically based on theories from more economically developed regions.

As activist Shweta Singh explains in 'Transgression into "Hidden" Feminisn: Immigrant Muslim Women from India' in *Feminism and Migration* (2012), advocating on a global scale for women's rights or shifts in gender roles is problematic 'both because society is collectivist, and because women them-selves identify with group concerns of family and community and not solely with womanhood or sisterhood'. In 2003 feminist writer Chandra Talpade Mohanty (b. 1955) critiqued Western feminism for constructing a homogenous category of 'Third-World women'. This category, she argues, bypasses the differences among and between women from less economically developed countries and thus fails to give a voice to women facing different struggles emerging around history, geography and culture – a problem that intersectional feminism aims to address (see Chapter 3).

A   Women march down
    Constitution Avenue on
    21 January 2017, the day after
    Donald Trump's Inauguration.
    Some 470,000 marchers
    protested against the impact
    of Trump's presidency on
    women's rights. The placard
    points to the marginalization
    of women of colour in the
    feminist movement.
B   Semerian Janet Pere, 17,
    reads inside a classroom
    at the Tasaru Safehouse
    for Girls in Narok, Kenya.
    The safehouse was opened
    in 2002 for girls fleeing FGM
    or child marriage.

Central issues here relate to religious practices and cultural traditions, including the wearing of the veil, marriage customs, sex work and practices of genital cutting – all of which are relevant to gender roles in various countries. The campaign Stop FGM Now!, headed by Waris Dirie (b. 1965), organizes as an international movement against female genital cutting, or, as it terms such practices, female genital mutilation. Other feminists such as Fuambai Sia Ahmadu (b. c. 1969) have, however, argued for the need to understand local experience of faith and tradition, and for campaigns to be led by local women themselves.

B

A

A   Members of the Femen activist group demonstrate at Berlin's oldest mosque, Ahmadiyya Moschee, in 2013. Under the slogan 'International Topless Jihad Day', they protested on behalf of Tunisian Femen activist Amina Tyler who received death threats after she posted topless photographs of herself online.
B   A counter protest was held by the group Muslim Women Against Femen. 'We as Muslim women and those who stand with us, need to show Femen and their supporters, that their actions are counterproductive and we as Muslim women oppose it,' they said.

Similar debates ensue about the wearing of the veil. From one feminist perspective, the veil is a symbol of male control over women's bodies; from another, veil wearing is an autonomous decision and a form of resistance to Western values, which makes the veil an emblem of cultural pride rather than a mark of male power.

Commenting on what he calls an 'obsession with clothing' in Western feminist and liberal discussions about the veil, journalist Faisal al Yafai writes in *The Guardian* (2008): 'The veil seems to be a real blind spot for some people, even for Western feminists, who appear to infantilize women who choose to wear the veil, even as they argue men have infantilized women in other areas. The idea that wearing a veil could be a free, rational choice appears to elude them.' Increasingly, young women such as Hanna Yusuf are using social media platforms to blog and vlog about their identities as hijab-wearing feminists.

# Intersectionality also covers the overlap between feminism and LGBTQ activism, trans theory and queer theory.

Feminism has been criticized for failing to take into account the experiences of those who do not subscribe to a binary model of gender; some feminist theorists – most famously Janice Raymond (b. 1943) – are actively opposed to the trans rights movement. Trans-exclusionary radical feminists, a small section of the feminist community, argue that trans women cannot truly identify as women due to the privilege inherent in their male upbringing.

B

LGBTQ and feminist movements have much common ground, however: both seek to problematize and challenge traditional assumptions about the workings of gender.

Trans writers, particularly from the 1990s onwards, have articulated identities that are consciously constructed against a binary model of gender.

Kate Bornstein (b. 1948), for example, in *Gender Outlaw* (1994), blows apart any categorization of sex as defined by genitalia: 'Most folks would define a man by the presence of a penis or some form of penis. Some would define a woman by the presence of a vagina or some form of vagina. It's not that simple though. I know several women in San Francisco who have penises. Many wonderful men in my life have vaginas. And there are quite a few people whose genitals fall somewhere between penises and vaginas.' Bornstein articulates herself not as in the 'wrong body', nor as belonging to a 'third sex', but as a 'gender outlaw'.

In *Whipping Girl* (2007), trans feminist theorist Julia Serano (b. 1967) positions both transphobia and homophobia as rooted in oppositional sexism, which she contrasts with traditional sexism, the idea that 'femininity is subordinate to masculinity'. Serano's work highlights the extent to which trans theory can illuminate issues affecting people of all genders, and underscores the ways in which the trans rights movement and the feminist movement can align.

## In addition to questioning traditional understandings of gender, trans activism focuses on the problems specifically faced by gender-diverse people across the world.

The Trans Murder Monitoring project provides global data on the murders of trans and gender-diverse people, publishing updated statistics on the Transgender Day of Remembrance, held on 20 November each year. Globally, there were 325 reported murders of trans and gender-diverse people between October 2016 and September 2017 alone. The number of reported murders is highest in countries with a monitoring system in place for such killings, suggesting a lack of data from other countries; it is therefore likely that many more murders go unreported. Publicly memorializing those who have lost their lives helps to highlight and condemn the hate crimes perpetrated against trans and gender-diverse people.

**Transphobia** is fear, dislike, prejudice or negative attitude directed towards transgender people.

**Oppositional sexism** identifies sexism associated with the idea that the categories of male and female are fixed and opposite, with 'each possessing a unique and non-overlapping set of attributes, aptitudes, abilities and desires'.

A    A vigil is held at the State University of Manila on 24 October 2014 to honour Jennifer Laude, a trans woman who was brutally murdered.
B    Westboro Baptist Church members protest at Ground Zero. They believe that terrorist acts are God's punishment to the world for homosexuality and sexual and gendered immorality.
C    Equality House in Topeka, Kansas, sits directly opposite Westboro Baptist Church. It is painted in rainbow colours in tribute to the gay pride flag.

# In addition to the risk of hate crime, trans and gender-diverse people often face a range of different types of institutional and individual discrimination.

These can range from violence – sometimes even perpetuated by government employees or police – to misgendering; missing or misleading representation in the media; and a disproportionately high risk of homelessness and unemployment. Particularly visible instances of institutional and legal discrimination in the USA have recently centred around bathroom bills and the right of transgender people to enlist in the US military.

Organizations such as Global Action for Trans* Equality, Wipe Out Transphobia and GLAAD work to support trans, gender-diverse and intersex causes, advocating for all gender identities to be depathologized; for legal and institutional frameworks that support the rights of all people; and for better education and awareness about gender diversity. Modern-day activism also takes

A

**Misgendering** refers to addressing a person with a pronoun or other term that does not correctly reflect their gender identity.

**Bathroom bills** are pieces of legislation that define gendered access to public bathrooms. They usually aim to prevent transgender people from accessing public facilities that cater for their affirmed gender.

A    *Tangerine* explores trans street culture. It focuses on two trans women, played by trans actors, who are trying to survive on the streets of Los Angeles. The film was shot on an iPhone 5s and premiered in 2015 at the Sundance Film Festival. In recent years, media representations of trans experiences have become more diverse and garnered more attention from the cultural mainstream.

B    Contestants line up for *RuPaul's Drag Race: All Stars*. A spin-off of the popular *RuPaul's Drag Race*, the show features drag queens competing for a place in the Drag Race Hall of Fame.

B

place on an individual level, with social media and other online activity playing an important part. Beyond this, each person who chooses to display gendered agency contributes a little to changing attitudes, widening acceptance of gender diversity, and encouraging individuals and communities to question the gender norms many have taken for granted.

# Instances of violence and discrimination need to be recognized, but activism has led to positive change in a number of areas.

There has been a significant shift in many countries away from understanding gender as a binary configuration that recognizes only male and female categories. A 2016 study by the British Fawcett Society found that 68% of young people believe gender is non-binary, whereas half of young people in the USA surveyed said that they do not see gender as limited to only male and female categories.

A

Shifting understandings and experiences of gender are feeding into everyday language. Non-binary personal pronouns such as the singular 'they' or 'their' are becoming more common among young people, and the term 'genderfluid' entered the Oxford Dictionary in 2016 to define a person who does not identify with a single fixed gender. Gender-neutral toilets are common in British universities and Speaker of the House of Commons John Bercow is pressing for non-gendered toilets in the Houses of Parliament in London.

# The effects of activism have reached the retail and media sectors, and representations of non-binary gender are increasingly widespread.

The popular video game 'Sims' has introduced gender-diverse characters, and trans characters have been portrayed numerously in television and film. Facebook has also recently launched multiple gender 'options' for its users. Companies such as JW Anderson, Rick Owens, Zara and H&M offer gender-neutral clothing. GFW (Gender Free World) Clothing creates shirts in three fits for different shaped bodies rather than for different genders, and The Butch Clothing Company designs clothes for masculine women.

Reflecting these socio-cultural changes and the dramatic rise in the cultural visibility of people who identify across, between or beyond the categories of male and female, *Time* magazine heralded a 'Transgender Tipping Point' in 2014. A year later, 2015 was declared the 'Year of Transgender' by media sources (BBC News, CNN News) in both Britain and the USA.

In its end of year pronouncement for 2015, the *Financial Times* stated: 'Year in a word: Trans: Gender discussion becomes a nuanced, fluid, "non-binary" affair.'

Significant cultural commentary has been devoted to the wider ramifications of the Year of Transgender on young people. Media reports in Britain and the USA, in *The Guardian* and *Teen Vogue*, for example, regularly declare that the millennial generation – or generation Y – are rejecting traditional gender labels and norms.

There is much evidence, then, to suggest that traditional gender identities and expressions are being less rigidly experienced, especially by young people in contemporary society, particularly – although not uniquely – in the West. Correspondingly, issues of equality for gender-diverse people have emerged on the political agenda in many countries, and recent years have witnessed greater legal protection for their rights.

A

A   Emma Watson (left) accepts the Best Actor in a Movie award for *Beauty and the Beast* from non-binary *Billions* actor Asia Kate Dillon at the 2017 MTV Movie & TV Awards at the Shrine Auditorium in Los Angeles. The event was significant for its introduction of gender neutral awards.
B   Transgender woman Wendy Iriepa and gay man Ignacio Estrada wave a gay pride flag as they leave in a vintage car after getting married on 13 August 2011 in Havana, Cuba. Iriepa's gender reassignment surgery was paid for by the Cuban state.

In Britain, the Gender Recognition Act of 2004 granted trans people the right to change their birth certificates and to marry in their acquired gender. Laws recognizing the acquired gender of trans people have been enacted in Croatia, the Czech Republic, Denmark, Finland, France, Germany, Ireland, Italy, the Netherlands, Norway, Poland, Portugal, Romania, Sweden and Spain. Outside Europe, transgender recognition legislation has been introduced in Brazil, Canada, Columbia, Ecuador, Iran, Japan, South Africa, Uruguay, India, Bangladesh and Vietnam. In 2012, Argentina was lauded as the world's most trans-friendly country when it declared that one's official gender may be changed on the basis of self-declaration, rather than on the authority of medical or legal professionals. In November 2017, a German court ruled that people who identify as neither male nor female, including intersex people, can be officially registered as a third gender.

# These discussions raise an important question about the future of gender. Are we moving towards a genderless world?

# Conclusion

A

Core beliefs are deep-seated understandings and assumptions about ourselves, others and how the world around us works. They are often subconsciously held, and can be difficult to recognize and change.

Some of our deepest core beliefs and the most fundamental structures of our cultures are built around gender, making it one of the central ways we categorize each other. We base a huge number of social roles and expectations on gender, from who 'should' undertake childcare or leadership roles to who 'should' wear certain items of clothing, enjoy certain hobbies or even experience certain feelings.

But gender is not always a solid basis for such categorization.

Each facet of gender, whether it be physical aspects, social role or personal identity, is subject to change, from society to society, from person to person, or even within the same person at different times.

Chapter 1 examined biological perspectives of gender, which present the categories of male and female as genetically determined and thus fixed. However, biological gender is complex and does not always fall discretely into male or female. In addition, gender is experienced and practised in ways that are much more intricate than a biological approach can account for.

The socially constructed elements of gender were considered in Chapter 2, using examples from different times, places and societies to show that gender roles are subject to change. Norms and values around gender are created by a range of intersecting factors, including politics, economics, religion, faith, social class, race and ethnicity.

A US heavyweight boxer Muhammad Ali cradles his daughter Laila after his championship victory over Leon Spinks in 1978.
B Pregnancy is no barrier for Alysia Montaño, who waits to run in the opening round of the women's 800 metres at the 2014 USATF Outdoor Championships at Hornet Stadium in Sacramento, California.

A

A    Pakistani trans women hold a vigil beside the body of transgender activist Alisha, who was shot by unknown gunmen in Peshawar in 2016. At the hospital, staff could not decide which ward to place her in and reports suggest that these delays contributed to her death.

B    A collage of tributes to 18-year-old Angie Zapata, who was brutally murdered in 2008 by Allen Andrade after he found out that she was a trans woman. He was the first person in the USA convicted of a hate crime involving a transgender victim.

Gender socialization shapes the way each person performs their gender. The roles we expect people to play based on their gender are therefore not consistent over time or between different cultures and communities.

In Chapter 3, gender-diverse practices and identities were explored in detail. We saw that there have always been people whose gender identities are diverse, but they are sometimes referred to in different ways or understood through different scientific and social models, depending on historical and cultural context.

Chapter 3 began to explore the problems of a binary model of gender for people who identify across, between or beyond the traditional male/female categories. Gender-diverse people in some non-Western countries have a long history of being socially integrated, while in others, social and cultural understandings, representations, and laws and policy are now broadening to take greater account of people who live outside of a gender binary. Correspondingly, there is a greater range of options for expressing gender open to many people today. These social changes emphasize the fact that gender is ever-evolving.

# Despite important changes across the globe to social attitudes, cultural visibility, and law and policy about transgender, trans people and gender non-binary people still face barriers.

Many countries have not yet legislated for trans recognition, and across those that have, the majority maintain a framework wherein trans people have to be certified as such by psychiatric professionals. Trans is still pathologized across much of the world. Self-harm and suicide among trans people, particularly the young, is disproportionately higher than among non-trans people. Discrimination in the workplace remains common. Trans people face harassment and violence within their families and in public. Murders of trans people, particularly trans women of colour, are numerous – and, disturbingly, are sometimes justified using the legal trans panic defence.

**Trans panic defence** is a legal defence in which the perpetrator of a crime (usually violent) claims in court that they lost self-control as a result of panic caused by their victim's transgender identity. Such defences have been used numerously in the USA, during the trial for the rape and murder of trans man Brandon Teena in 2003, for example.

A

Cisgender men and women, as well as trans and non-binary people, can find that their options are restricted by social expectations about what roles they can perform. Men are often expected to limit their emotional range and expression; to provide financially for their families; to face or even commit physical violence in order to maintain their social status; or to choose work commitments over involvement in childcare. Women face a wide range of problems, from high risks of poverty, harassment and sexual violence, to lack of education, reproductive rights and adequate healthcare, to forced marriage, workplace discrimination and the gender wage gap.

As Chapter 4 described, gendered inequalities have been the subject of activism and campaigning by feminists, egalitarians, men's rights activists and trans activists throughout the world.

Although gender operates as a structuring device that limits the lives of women, men and non-binary people, it also operates as a site of agency in which individuals or groups can work to reshape their gendered practices, impacting changing understandings of gender.

It is evident that an understanding of gender as diverse is not universal; many people continue to argue that gender is 'hard-wired'. But by looking at the range of approaches to and practices of gender in existence, both today and throughout human history, we can see clearly that gender is not a fixed attribute. What is more, at the disjuncture between traditionally gendered social roles and everyday gendered experiences emerges a site of systemic injustice against trans people, gender-diverse people and cisgender people, which limits individual and collective potential.

# The world we live in remains far from gender neutral, but moves towards gender fluidity are to be welcomed. They enable greater possibilities for all.

**Egalitarians** believe that all humans are equal in worth and should be treated equally by society, regardless of gender, sexuality, race, religion, ability, class or political affiliation.

**Systemic injustice** is injustice that is inherent to a particular social, economic or political system, meaning that it is automatically perpetuated by that system.

# Picture Credits

Every effort has been made to locate and credit copyright holders of the material reproduced in this book. The author and publisher apologize for any omissions or errors, which can be corrected in future editions.

a=above, b=below, c=centre, l=left, r=right

71 © Shirin Neshat

72 baolamdong.vn

73l Photo Reza/Getty Images

73r Photo Rod Aydelotte-Pool/
Getty Images

74 Landsberger collection
(BG E13/415)

75 Photo VCG via Getty Images

76–77 Trinity Mirror/Mirrorpix/
Alamy Stock Photo

78l, 78r nsf/Alamy Stock Photo

79 Chronicle/Alamy Stock Photo

80 Photo Shaul Schwarz/Getty
Images

81 Photo Ulet Ifansasti/Getty
Images

82 Photo Allison Joyce/Getty
Images

83 Photo Mohammad Asad/
Pacific Press/LightRocket
via Getty Images

84a, 84b, 85a, 85b Wellcome
Collection, London

86l Photo Corbis via Getty Images

86r Musée des Beaux-Arts
de Nantes

87 Photo Fox Photos/Getty Images

88 Magnus-Hirschfeld-
Gesellschaft, Berlin

89 Photo by Weegee (Arthur Fellig)
/International Center of
Photography/Getty Images

90 Photo Michael Maslan/
Corbis/VCG via Getty Images

91 Frederick Richard Pickersgill

92 Yale Center for British Art,
Paul Mellon Collection
(B1977.14.11245)

93l Wellcome Collection, London

93r Gerda Wegener, 1928

94 Photo Hulton-Deutsch
Collection/Corbis via
Getty Images

95 Bettmann/Getty Images

96l Alfred C. Kinsey, Wardell B.
Pomeroy, Clyde E. Martin,
Sexual Behaviour in the
Human Male, W.B. Saunders,
Philadelphia, 1948

96c Alfred C. Kinsey, Wardell B.
Pomeroy, Clyde E. Martin, Paul

H. Gebhard, Sexual Behaviour
in the Human Female, W.B.
Saunders, Philadelphia, 1953

96r Dr. Murray Banks, What
You Can Learn From The
Kinsey Report, 1956. Audio
Mastertone Label by Froco
Records

97l, 97r Lawrence Lariar, OH!
DR. KINSEY!; A Photographic
Reaction to the Kinsey Report,
Cartwrite Publishing Co,
New York, 1953

98, 99 Illustrations Daniel Street,
Visual Fields 100l, 100r Trinity
Mirror/Mirrorpix/Alamy

101 Photo David Levenson/
Getty Images

102l, 102r, 103l, 103r © Sarah Wong

104 Reuters/Brendan McDermid

105 Dial Books, 2015. Penguin
Books

106–107 Photo Michael Nigro/
Pacific Press/LightRocket
via Getty Images

108 Musée Carnavalet,
Paris (D.9092). Photo
Roger-Viollet/Topfoto

109l Brooklyn Museum, Gift
of Emily Winthrop Miles
(55.9.25v)

109r AF Fotografie/Alamy Stock
Photo

110l Schomburg Center for
Research in Black Culture.
Photographs and Prints
Division. The New York
Public Library

110r Prints and Photographs
Division, Library of Congress,
Washington, D.C.

111 Prints and Photographs
Division, Library of Congress,
Washington, D.C.

112 Photo Barbara Freeman/
Getty Images

113l, 113c, 113r Courtesy
University of Victoria
Libraries, Transgender
Archives (HQ77 T73)

114l, 114r Kathleen Hanna

(Bikini Kill) at the Macondo,
Los Angeles, 1993

115 Photo Rick Kern/Wirelmage

116al, 116bl, 116ar, 116br Courtesy
Top-Toy

117 John Lewis campaign,
Charlie Smith Design

118 © Kevin Banatte @
afroCHuBBZ and Angela
Marie @MsPeoples

119 Photo Marvi Lacar/
Getty Images

120 Photo Target Presse Agentur
Gmbh/Getty Images

121 Muslima Pride International

122 Photo Ted Aljibe/AFP/
Getty Images

123a Photo Monika Graff/
Getty Images

123b Photo Mark Reinstein/
Corbis via Getty Images

124 Film poster, Tangerine,
dir. Sean Baker, 2015

125 Photo Jamie McCarthy/
Getty Images

126 Time Inc/Meredith Corporation

127l Photo Gareth Cattermole/
Getty Images for MTV
Crashes Glasgow

127r Photo Jason Squires/
Wirelmage

128 Photo Kevin Winter/
Getty Images

129 Photo Sven Creutzmann/
Mambo Photo/Getty Images

130 Musée du Louvre, Paris.
Photo RMN-Grand Palais
(musée du Louvre)/Hervé
Lewandowski

132 Photo Chuck Fishman/
Getty Images

133 Photo Andy Lyons/Getty
Images

134 Arshad Arbab/Epa/REX/
Shutterstock

135 Photo Joe Amon/The Denver
Post via Getty Images

136 Photo Bradley Felstead

137a, b Photo Romy Arroyo
Fernandez/NurPhoto via
Getty Images

# Index

References to illustrations
are in **bold**.

Acknowledgments:
The author would like to thank the editorial team
at Thames & Hudson for their enthusiasm for
this project. Special thanks – and love – go
to Gil Jackson-Hines, the master of debate.

First published in the United Kingdom in 2018
by Thames & Hudson Ltd, 181A High Holborn,
London WC1V 7QX

*Is Gender Fluid?* © 2018
Thames & Hudson Ltd, London

General Editor: Matthew Taylor
Text by Sally Hines

For image copyright information, see pp. 138–139

British Library Cataloguing-in-Publication Data
A catalogue record for this book is available from
the British Library

ISBN 978-0-500-29368-3

Printed and bound in Hong Kong through Asia
Pacific Offset Ltd

To find out about all our publications,
please visit **www.thamesandhudson.com**.
There you can subscribe to our e-newsletter,
browse or download our current catalogue,
and buy any titles that are in print.